Classroom Experiences

The Writing Process in Action

Edited by

Naomi M. Gordon

Heinemann Educational Books
Exeter, New Hampshire

Heinemann Educational Books Inc.
4 Front Street, Exeter, New Hampshire 03833

LONDON   EDINBURGH   MELBOURNE   AUCKLAND
HONG KONG   SINGAPORE   KUALA LUMPUR
NEW DELHI   IBADAN   NAIROBI   JOHANNESBURG
KINGSTON   PORT OF SPAIN

Cover design by Ryan Cooper
Photo credits
Front cover, top to bottom, left to right
Judith E. Kostin, Ilene Salo-Miller, Judith E. Kostin, Marla McCurdy,
Marla McCurdy
Back cover, top to bottom
Judith E. Kostin, Marla McCurdy

Library of Congress cataloging in Publication Data
Main entry under title:

Classroom experiences.

    1. English language—Composition and exercises—
Addresses, essays, lectures. I. Gordon, Naomi.
LB1576.C5634   1984   372.6'23   84-6560
ISBN 0-435-08210-8

Printed in the United States of America

CONTENTS

The Authors

The seven contributors to *Classroom Experiences* are teachers in the Brookline, Massachusetts, public schools. They have a wide variety of educational and career backgrounds, and all are involved in day-to-day classroom teaching.

(l to r) Standing: Naomi Gordon, Elementary Coordinator for Language Arts; Marla McCurdy, first grade teacher; Seymour Yesner, high school English teacher. Seated: Ilene Salo-Miller, fourth grade teacher; Cynthia Bencal, sixth grade teacher; Deborah D'Amico, second grade teacher, Evelyn Lerman, seventh grade teacher, Vice Principal, Baker School.

Introduction

Seymour Yesner

With so many books and articles already produced about the writing process, what makes this book necessary and unique?

Its uniqueness originates in its writers, all but one classroom teachers in the Brookline, Massachusetts elementary schools, and all experienced teachers who came to the process skeptically, but by virtue of their natures, experimentally. These were not teachers seeking change for its own sake, but teachers who constantly tried for better ways to teach and found that the writing process accomplished what they deemed important in the teaching of writing, and also happily improved their students' writing.

This book, as a compendium of teacher recollections about their own struggles and growth, will find among other teachers an immediate recognition of common problems and concerns. It also will offer to teachers a special insight into a process that could help them try out different approaches to writing in grades K–8.

It would be wrong to see the chapters of this book as blueprints to be followed precisely. The book does not provide a sequence of writing skills nor a prescriptive set of writing exercises, though it does show in considerable detail the methods, organization, and activities that the teachers used. Mainly, it presents improvisational possibilities and ideas that teachers who read it can adapt according to their own inventive tendencies.

There is a tentative quality about this book probably because no assertions are made as absolutes. This tentative quality exists not because the teacher-authors lack self-assurance, but because they see the process they are describing as a continuous adaptation to the changing demands of their students and as a projection of a particular teacher's style and temperament. You are receiving the anecdotal reflections of very competent practitioners about how they altered their manner of teaching, the frustrations and skepticism they often felt, their need for support to prevent reverting to more comfortable and secure practices, and the successes and failures they experienced. It is the process of their change that is central to this book.

Initially, the change seems to signify a diminished role for the teacher. It appears so because the teacher is no longer the final word, the ultimate corrector, the dispenser of irrefutable wisdom, the bestower or withholder of gold stars, the elevator or depressor of young egos. Instead, he or she is an audience, a reactor, and an interactor who shares perceptions and experiences with the students, and often participates in the process by writing, by sharing this writing with the students, and by accepting their remarks. As a result, the teacher achieves a changed and more significant function.

First, this change does not exclude what teachers in general know to be important in developing a writing environment and a writing psyche. They know that students need to do a considerable amount of writing, be aware of whom they are writing for, be able to conform to certain conventions, and, most important, be eager to express themselves. In this regard, the change can be construed as a natural extension of what in all probability is already sought after. Where the change occurs as a real departure is in how the classroom becomes a writing laboratory, a place where writing goes on continuously and with considerable pleasure because of the interaction between and among all members of the class, including the teacher. What we now refer to as "the writing process" offers, in addition, several improvements because it starts students writing earlier and introduces them and the teacher to a more realistic procedure for using writing as a tool, one that corresponds more closely to what working writers do. It also makes writing intrinsic to all learning in the classroom, a natural mode for expressing oneself, and a means for explaining and exploring ideas—in other words, a problem-solving device that demands interaction with other students and the teacher.

Second, and most important, the move toward change is intellectually inspiring. It offers teachers insights into the function of language in general and writing in particular. It focuses their pedagogy on how students develop language proficiency so that instruction corresponds to that development.

Last, the evolving changes in teaching style and in expectation produce their own momentum that once started probably will not stop. Teachers using this process tend to become more self-analytical and self-critical. They become more attuned to language nuances both in talking to their students about the writing being produced and in examining that writing. They use student exchanges more, perfect conference strategies, and trust students to develop their own topics and to judge their own limits of endurance with a particular project. Teachers also find that they can embellish their own, often unique, results through ongoing exchanges with each other. What is started here should never end. The flow of ideas from teachers and students in an ever-changing world merge to produce torrents of words in the never-ending struggle to express oneself.

What works in Brookline can work anywhere if certain conditions are met. These conditions are surprisingly uncomplicated yet often create major obstacles to the success of any writing venture. For instance, teachers need to be able to work together and support each other, especially when the going gets rough; parents need to be informed about what is happening in writing so they can understand and not become antagonistic; principals, school committee people, other teachers, and the general community need to be kept informed so that they can be cooperative and can see to it that appropriate provisions (necessary materials, manageable class sizes, and adequate time allotments) are made to insure the success of the program and to serve as concrete evidence that improvement in writing is considered important.

The teachers who have written this book discovered a shared enthusiasm for what they are doing, a sense of success, and a marvelous reciprocity in learning from each other. It is this learning they now wish to share with others. The book itself unfolds as a chapter by chapter case study of how teachers at particular grade levels interpreted a process and put it into practice. Each case study reveals the necessity for insight into youngsters—their capacities for learning, their interests, their ability to sustain an activity. Each study reveals the full range of problems and possibilities.

There are *five teacher chapters* written by teachers of the following grades: Grades K–1, Grades 2–3, Grade 4, Grade 6, and Grades 7–8. Each chapter describes the essentials of the writing process. The features include the steps of the process itself as well as the management issues that arise at each grade level. Each chapter has its own flavor, order and emphasis, and each chapter includes the following information:

1. Getting Ready and Setting Up the Environment
   The teacher introduces different ways of preparing the students to write. Various activities and examples of how to manage the process are given.
2. Getting Started
   Procedures for rehearsals, warm-ups, talking about topics, and selecting a topic are provided.
3. Writing
   The writing begins. The idea that children write about a topic which they strongly know and care about is discussed.
4. Possession.
   Teachers are made aware that students become the authors and own the stories they write: students make the final decisions in editing and revising.
5. Conferences
   This feature gives suggestions for ways to help students learn to share and talk about their written work with others. Through "conferencing," students gain insights and develop new ideas to enhance their stories.
6. Drafting and Revising
   Teachers give students the opportunity to rework their stories. The students make changes, eliminating unnecessary parts and adding information or details.
7. Proofreading
   Different methods for handling the process of proofreading are introduced.
8. Problems and frustrations
   Problems that arise during the writing process are mentioned and some methods for handling these problems are given. Anecdotes and actual classroom situations are included.
9. Mechanics, Grammar, Spelling, and Usage
   Emphases vary with grade level. Some suggestions for developing language skills and mastering the conventions of writing are included.

10. "Publishing"
    Students decide whether they wish to complete their written story in the form of a published work. These works are then available to be read by other students and teachers—and of course, by parents.
11. Evaluating
    Some suggestions are given for dealing with what kind of written work can be expected from students at different stages of their development.

As will be seen, each chapter deals with the specifics of the writing process in the context of the broader aspects of the process. Thus, a chapter emphasizing prewriting shows how a particular teacher at a particular grade level works with students in this phase of the overall writing process, even though all other features of the process are addressed as well.

It should be noted that each phase meshes with other phases and should not be regarded as a distinct operation. Though "the conference" can be seen as a discrete phase in the total process, it obviously can occur at any phase. For instance, a teacher may confer with a student to get him *started*, or two students may confer to get one or both of them *started*, or people in a classroom can confer during the various *revising* phases.

Considerable credit must be given to Donald Graves, his colleagues such as Lucy Calkins, and the staff at Atkinson Academy, Atkinson, New Hampshire, who employed methods espoused by Graves and who confirmed for us, after visits by many of our teachers, what had already been a speculative viewpoint: that the young—even the very young—can begin to write, can write lucidly with appropriate help and conditions, can express themselves with joy and honesty in writing, and can use writing as a tool for intellectual development, especially if given control over topic choice, assistance in developing a focus, and encouragement to rewrite—that is, to rethink and reshape—with an audience in mind.

Additional credit for propelling us into this process needs to go to the host of theorists and proponents of new and better ways to engage students in learning to write. Though we could reach back for our foundations to Dora V. Smith and perhaps even earlier to Meader, the contemporary impetus, as we see it, emerged from the Dartmouth Conference and the work of such people as John Dixon, James Britten, and James Moffett. Coming also immediately to mind is the work of Janet Emig, Lee Odell, Charles Cooper, Stephen Judy, Donald Murray, Ken Macrorie, Peter Elbow, James Gray, and Richard Lloyd-Jones. We acknowledge our debt to all of them and to the many others who, though unnamed, have helped improve our work in the classroom.

1. Writing on Their Own: Kindergarten and First Grade

Marla McCurdy

Before you read this chapter, look at the message below and guess what it says:

> N m V₂ WT+ m CS hs

Fill in your response in the box right now. You will discover what it says at a later point.

"How do you spell 'the'?" "How do you spell 'they'?" "How do you spell? . . . spell? . . . spell?" Writing experiences for my K/1 classroom seemed to consist only of many nonreaders flocking to me to get the correct spelling for whatever words they wished to write down. Their resulting stories were good—but were they really theirs? Or were they only combinations of their thoughts and lots of input from me? There must be a better way! How can a teacher reinforce the impetus to begin writing without extinguishing motivation through excessive attention to spelling, punctuation, and grammatical errors? In writing tasks where this type of attention is given, beginners—eager at the start—end up writing less. Fear of mistakes and the tedium of correction stunts the imaginative quality of children's writing and limits the quantity of material they produce.

These thoughts were constantly with me during the opening months of my first year as a K/1 teacher. Previously, for four years as a kindergarten teacher, I had used the word box approach to writing, in which children learn words from cards filed in boxes. As their word cards multiply, they are able to put sentences together and gradually, short stories. As a group the children and I wrote experience stories about field trips and other classroom happenings. We spent considerable time on expressing ideas and thoughts in full sentences and placing them in sequential order. These writing readiness skills were useful and worked well in leading to independent writing. In the kindergarten setting, the word box approach was both appropriate and successful. Transferred to my present situation, however, this approach for individual writing was not practical. I now had a classroom of twenty-four children at two levels, kindergarten and first grade. Their diversity—in reading ability, spelling, and grammar skills—made the word box approach to writing unmanageable. I was unable to meet the daily needs of all the children, and their writing would end up at a standstill until I could find time to help them. It seemed to me that there must be a way to introduce writing that would get even nonreaders writing spontaneously with a minimum of teacher help.

Then came the day when I attended a workshop on "The Writing Process," offered by the language arts department. I listened with dawning hope to the description of a process which encouraged children to write their own "invented spelling." "Let them spell their own way! . . . don't give them the correct spelling! . . . let them spell by writing down the sounds they hear!" This idea seemed an answer to much of my uneasiness with the writing that was going on in my classroom. Would it really work?

Getting Started

The next morning I gathered the first grade children together and suggested that they tell *me* how to spell some words rather than my telling *them*. We started with a simple sentence:

The dog chased the cat.

Taken word by word, the sentence came out:

a   dg   sd   a   ct

We did several sentences like this. Then I announced to the children that, from now on, when they did their writing, they were to try and write down their own words without asking me how to spell them. I included other things for them to try and remember:

(1) Space the words. Put two fingers beside each word before starting the next word or put a dash between each word.
(2) Write from left to right.

Then I let them go.

Initially there were those children who felt very uneasy about "spelling" by themselves. "Is this right?" several kept asking, while others went quickly ahead and wrote things down. But the result was sometimes impossible for me to read:

$$M \: d \quad G O \: P P S \tag{1}$$

Help! How was I supposed to decipher that (translations are given at the end of the chapter)? Furthermore, when I asked the child to read it back to me, he gazed at the letters and said, "I don't know." He looked just as confused as I felt. Maybe this approach would not work after all.

I went back and reread the articles and selections on the process approach to writing which I had obtained at the initial workshop, and then went through my children's writing again. Individual patterns began to emerge. Some words consisted of just beginning and ending consonants, others of beginning, ending, and medial consonants. Each child's ability to produce decipherable writing seemed to be tied to his reading ability. For instance, the writing of a nonreading child looked like this:

$$B G G B \quad \underset{FN S}{\overset{MP}{}} \quad \overset{9}{} \overset{Z}{} \: IMIN \: ar$$

Luckily, I was able to get to him just as he finished writing this sentence. Translated it means, "This is my imaginary friend, Bgooga." At this point the "nonreader" was actually reading his own material. The theory that all children had to be taught to read well before they could be expected to write began to seem refutable. I was seeing and hearing evidence to the contrary.

A child reading on the first Preprimer level presented a sentence more easily understood:

$$AND \: I \: SAW \: A \: LION \: HE \: ASK \: ME \\ ME \: NAM \: WS \: ABBY \tag{2}$$

I could easily read that! Encouraged, I sifted through the pile of children's writing books—each made of three sheets of lined paper folded in half and stapled, with a construction paper cover. I found a passage in one by a child reading on a third Preprimer level which read:

We WeNT To MRS.
WeN we got theAR.
We SAW MR ShiNS   (3)

This excerpt was even more encouraging. The writing pieces became easier for me to read as the child's level of reading skill grew. I could definitely see clear, decipherable results from the children who had some reading ability. They were writing comfortably and independently. But what about the nonreading children? Should I discontinue this process with them?

I formed a group of first graders who were struggling with the beginning phonics of putting *m   a   t* together and sounding out 'mat.' Very slowly, as their blending ability improved, I also began to see a real improvement in several other things: (1) increased ease in putting down letter symbols to represent words, (2) less dependence on asking me if they did it right and, greatest of all, (3) more skill on my part in interpreting their writing easily and reinforcing their progress.

Practice at reading invented spelling actually made the task easier and easier for all of us. Encouraged by this growth in both the children and me, I decided to make a real commitment to this writing process. The children were writing on a daily basis, and it was clear that they did not have to wait to be "ready to read" before beginning to write. The only part of the program I was still uneasy about was how to explain the process to parents, although, as I will explain later, it proved to be much easier than I thought.

Setting up the Environment

One of the first things I did to make it evident to the children that I considered writing an integral part of each day was to create a "storybook corner." This was a place where the children's in-progress and new storybooks were kept. Each first-grade child had a pocket made from a manila folder and labelled with his name and the word *Storybook* in which to store his writing-in-progress. New books, made from lined paper and construction paper, were also kept there, ready for use. The children were expected to write every day—as little or as much as they desired. Especially at the beginning, the amount each one wrote varied with the ease each one felt with the process. Kindergarten children were quick to ask if they could have a folder too and I quickly saw that the process was "catching." The younger children felt that they were "grown up," more competent, and in fact, were excited about doing the same kind of "work" as the first graders.

Since that first year, I have always introduced the invented spelling technique to the kindergarten children in the K/1 class as well as to the first graders. In many cases, I needed only to praise their own first attempts to write in order to get the process started.

I found that further interest in a storybook or writing area could be encouraged by including various kinds of paper, small composition books, "nice" pencils (with erasers), felt tip pens for making illustrations, and book covers for "publishing" the finished product (I will discuss the publishing process later). It proved to be important to me for organizational purposes that the children put their current writing project in their storybook pocket. That way I was easily able to keep track of what piece of writing each child was working on. As each piece was "finished" in the child's view, the selection was placed in a "finished work" box. When I found time during the day to read the completed work, I did so—often only after the children had gone home.

My next task was to discover a way to talk with an individual child about his writing during the day. In working with little children, I have found that there is rarely time during the school day when I am free to talk leisurely with one child. Our language arts period had been set up so that each first-grade child had four tasks to do: language skill sheets, independent reading, handwriting, and writing. This arrangement meant that I was always needed—to answer questions, to check on completed work, and to suggest and direct children to other activities when they had completed assigned tasks.

To help with this problem, I revised the class schedule to contain a period for language arts skills and reading, and a separate amount of time for storybook writing. Kindergarteners were given the option of drawing or writing, and first graders were told they had to include writing, but were also encouraged to draw. This arrangement left me freer to help with the children's specific writing questions, such as

1. What should I write about?
2. Will you read my book?
3. Can I read my book to you?
4. What else can I say about my trip?

To increase the possibility of having someone available to make immediate notes directly on a child's writing, I made use of every able person I could locate: student teachers, instructional aides, third graders, or anyone else who was willing. The third graders in particular responded with enthusiasm and proved to be very accepting of and encouraging to the younger children. The beginning of the year when there were many nonreaders was the most crucial time to have these people available to help. As that year progressed and the children's reading abilities improved, we needed fewer helping hands. During the four ensuing years, as I became more comfortable with this process and more adept at translating, I did not need as many volunteers to help get it started. I found that it continued to be necessary, however, to translate nonreaders' writing as soon as possible and that this type of conference had to have priority.

Conferencing

Conferencing with kindergarten and first grade children centered around topic selection, and what ideas to include about a topic. Many children, when first starting their writing, produced several one-page "stories"—a drawing with one or two words or phrases. At first, it was important to accept these products to give the children positive reinforcement and encouragement to continue. But gradually I began to ask the children who turned in several of these dashed-off "stories" what else they could tell me, or another reader, about them. For instance, for this story:

When I go home I play with my dog.

suggestions could include such questions as:

1. What kind of dog is it?
2. What color is it?
3. What kind of games do you play with him?
4. How old is he?
5. What makes him special?

Or, such a story as:

I love Liz Mom Daddy I love Patty.
Liz love me Mom I Patty.
Mom. Mi Mom love me Patty.
Daddy. Mi Daddy love me Liz.

lends itself to such conference questions as:

1. What kinds of things do you like to do with your family?
2. Can you tell about one special thing you did?

Many children needed help in adding to what they wrote. They tended to get stuck in repetitious statements such as those in the second example. To lead children through the process of learning to make their thoughts more complete, it was often necessary to take one question a day and have a child express his answer in a complete sentence. Then the child wrote down exactly what he had said. For children who could read, I found that I could write similar questions directly into their story-books. It became evident after several days of the new work schedule that during the time when everyone was writing or drawing I had an opportunity to speak to a number of children about what they were doing, to make suggestions for topics, and to help make an already chosen topic more complete. (This time slot is easier in a solid first-grade class than in one which also includes kindergarteners, with their relatively short attention spans.) Conferencing has to be tailored to the individual child's readiness skills for reading and writing. I found that the ability to write in complete sentences, to spell with some accuracy, and to express complex ideas in sentence form were, once again, closely allied to the reading ability of a child.

My emphasis was, and still is, on getting ideas on to paper, not on neat handwriting. If messiness makes it impossible for me to read a paper, I call this fact to a child's attention in a conference; otherwise, exercises in handwriting take place separately. The children do little revision outside of expanding on their thoughts because I am convinced that the key to writing freely and unself-consciously lies in getting words onto paper at this very beginning stage. I have seen too many children freeze or tighten up when told it is writing time. Children need to feel that their writing will be accepted, that it is satisfactory, and that their teacher will like it. Too often adults decide for children what they are to write about. There is a place for assigned topic selection, but the flow of ideas needs to be loosened first. Children must establish their own authority over their own writing before they can be expected to write about topics that are not self-selected.

Writing Stages

As that first year progressed, it became clear that the children's ability to write developed through various stages. In the very beginning stage, the child's reading ability consisted of sounding out short vowel words such as *cat, dog, pat,* etc. and his sight vocabulary was nonexistent. The children were dependent at this stage, checking in often with me: "How do you write . . .?" Again and again I found myself asking, "What sounds do you hear?" and I would pronounce the word in question, and greatly exaggerate the beginning and ending consonant sounds. Their spelling consisted of beginning and ending consonants and occasionally, some short vowels. Their sentences did not always run along in a straight line and did not always go from left to right. The children's stories were choppy and nonsequential. Their thoughts were expressed incompletely, and it was often necessary for a child to talk aloud about what he was thinking in order to understand his story line. At this point, when it was crucial to have a child read what he had written before he forgot it, volunteers to write down sentences were very useful. Here is a sample of a child's writing at this first stage of development:

This is a SaSSp (4)

Samples from the second stage of writing development showed the use of beginning and ending consonants, and some short vowels. Children at this level were still decoding phonetically but their blending was faster, and they had mastered a beginning sight vocabulary.

The tigs hat LUK to rid buks tha hav som buks hat tha bot uos. (5)

Their stories had more consistent story lines and consecutive thoughts about the same subject were a little more defined. Stories were still short, five or six pages with one sentence each, and it was still necessary to have the child read aloud to me soon after he finished writing, but translation was much easier for me, and a period of time (as much as one day) could elapse before a reading took place. Constant dependence on me for reassurance was gone. Each child by now was feeling far more comfortable about writing alone.

By the time a child moved from strictly phonetic reading to reading with long vowels and possessing sight words on a Preprimer level, his writing selections had become more creative. At this third stage, children still had trouble putting together a whole story about a subject and making it more complete than: "The flower is pretty. It is white. I like flowers." However, I needed to make fewer suggestions because in most cases, the children knew what to write about, and were not dependent on me anymore as a backpatter.

Children's writing in this third stage now included words with beginning and ending consonants, medial consonants and many more short vowels. In addition, many short words were spelled correctly; e.g., *the, saw, fish, went, in, to,* and *got.* Children now could read their own work easily several days after writing it, and I had no trouble translating their work. Their reading ability had progressed to the last Preprimer level, and they possessed a good sight vocabulary, which was definitely and positively correlated to the increasing number of correctly spelled words in their writing. I could now pick up a page such as the following and read it:

Tat Was a SiDe
Tet Got BlonuP BaYe
a Amerekin Pahe
it WAsa Grmen siDe (6)

I no longer felt like calling "Help!" when I looked at writing samples. On the contrary, their sophistication encouraged me to stick with the nonreaders and their attempts at writing.

By the time I saw writing selections from children in a fourth stage of development, any leftover uneasiness with the process approach to writing left me. Their reading ability had progressed to a first and second Primer level and was smooth and fluent. Their increased retention of a sight vocabulary resulted in a greater amount of correct spelling. Their story lines were more developed and had definite subject matter. Writing was completely independent. Short vowels were always included, and blends and endings such as *sh, ch, in,* and *ed* appeared. A typical sample of this stage is this story:

Oer Trip toCALiKorniA

Ohce MY Sister haD a freNb her Name is LaurA PLAtt We Are goiing to VeZ it her

iN-FeBrUAry-AND-We Are ALSO. goiiNg to See Are NeNi AND grAMPA   (7)

Conferencing at this level could be very effectively done verbally or in writing on an individual basis. Reading to another child and interest in a friend's writing increased considerably. Children sometimes adopted ideas from someone else's stories. For instance, outer space vehicles and television programs were very popular subject materials.

Punctuation can be introduced most effectively during this fourth writing stage. Capital letters, periods, question marks, and exclamation points are the first concepts I introduce because using them makes the children's writing clearer to the reader and the children can readily see that this is so. These are followed by quotation marks and commas, which are rarely introduced at the first grade level because their correct and appropriate use is harder for the children to understand.

Children wrote more often about actual experiences at this stage. A logical, sequential recording of a family trip, such as the above selection, began to appear regularly.

Eliciting Genres

I also noticed that different forms of writing, other than imaginary stories and reports about actual happenings, began to appear in the children's storybooks. At this point, activities in science and social studies that required writing and recording took on a new dimension. The science program used in my school system asks for a significant amount of observation, investigation, and recording from children, particularly from first graders. Their facility with invented spelling made recording exercises much simpler. They felt calm and relaxed about recording their findings independently. In social studies, too, I found I could ask them for written summaries of the lessons and they were comfortable about doing it without a list of vocabularly words on the board.

Children spontaneously began to write poetry about their own interests. In most cases, the poems were simple and concentrated solely on rhyming words, but sometimes a child produced a rather profound piece of work. The following poem was written by a child in the third writing stage. It had taken her a long time to use the writing process for her own pleasure and to relax to a point where she was not concerned with "doing it right." Her efforts and their results pleased her enormously. When a visiting actor read her poem aloud to several classes, she positively beamed.

> How do flowers grow,
> How do flowers grow,
> Out of the earth,
> Did you know.
>
> But why do flowers grow,
> But why do flowers grow,
> To make the earth pretty,
> Did you know.
>
> But where do flowers grow,
> But where do flowers grow,
> In grassy spaces,
> Did you know.

Publishing

When a child was satisfied that his piece of writing was finished, he was ready to have his book "published." His story would be typed and then bound in a cover, which he picked out from wallpaper samples, file folders, or construction paper. (These are easy to make; however, they do take time! Parents can help here by making five or six covers for their child, to be kept in the classroom, ready for use, as their child completes a book.)

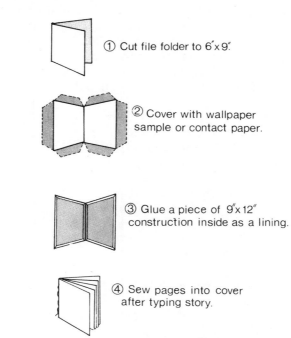

① Cut file folder to 6″x 9″.

② Cover with wallpaper sample or contact paper.

③ Glue a piece of 9″x 12″ construction inside as a lining.

④ Sew pages into cover after typing story.

A volunteer student teacher, a parent, or I myself typed the finished stories, keeping the exact format the child used but correcting all the spelling, and adding appropriate punctuation. It may seem that this published version of a child's writing, which changes his invented spelling to correct spelling and adds correct punctuation, is contrary to several previous statements I have made. For instance, I maintain that the children must establish their own authority over their own writing. Publishing the child's own format, but with corrections, seems opposed to this idea. But I do this because these published books are kept in the classroom for others to read. In a kindergarten or first grade classroom, most of the children are just learning to read. They are in the process of decoding and sounding out words phonetically. Their published books add to and create another dimension in the total reading program. Since no two children's invented spelling is at the same level of development at the same time, it would be very confusing to them as beginning readers to try to decipher each other's invented spelling in book form. The purpose of changing the spelling, then, is to make it consistent with other reading material used in the reading program.

For instance, the following story, spread over six pages:

The bike ride
wen I ride my bike i fall off a lot Twen
i was rideing my I fel off i huert my self
I fel on a roke Then i got up And fel dawn
a gaen. Then i got up and ride off i went
up hill and fel a gen. a hourt my self.
Then i got up a gen and rid off by myself.
Then i got on to the rode. Then i got on
to a big bump And then i got on to a big
bump. Then i got hom

would appear as follows in its typed form:

The Bike Ride

When I ride my bike, I fall off a lot.
When I was riding my bike, I fell off.
I hurt myself. I fell on a rock. Then
I got up and fell down again. Then I got
up and rode off. I went up hill and fell
again and hurt myself. Then I got onto
the road. Then I got into a big bump.
Then I got home.

The pages are then sewn into the cover and the book given back to the child, who can top off the published story with new illustrations. I provide felt-tip pens for this task, since they make the book more attractive, and give the children an added incentive to draw carefully. All the published books are then kept near the reading area so that during a library or reading period children can read each other's work. They did this extensively! I became increasingly surprised at the level of the children's interest in stories that had been published.

For me, the most delightful part of this end product was the immense pride that the children had in their books. They read their own over and over, took them home to share with their families, and brought their parents in to look at them and read them in the classroom. Every bit of the effort and time put into the process was rewarded by their pride and their feelings of achievement. Most important to me was knowing that these writing pieces were the children's own work. They had thought of, written down, and illustrated everything, with very little direction from me after the initial task of getting them started. As a teacher, I view myself as a facilitator and a provider in the classroom, and the process approach to writing fits in easily with this philosophy.

Illustrating

Drawings and illustrations are an important, integral part of the writing process. Children at a very young age start drawing with scribbles, lines, and marks on a page. At about age three and a half to four years, these marks evolve into pictures that are self-explanatory. By the time a child is in kindergarten, drawing is an activity consuming much of his time and effort and is used as a means of communication with other children and with adults.

Drawings as a part of writing seemed to fall roughly into three categories. At a beginning level, when writing words down on paper was still a difficult process, the drawings accompanying a piece of written material were complex and intricate, and were used as the chief means of "telling." For instance, an example of writing from a child who was reading at a Preprimer level looked like this:

The pictures are the chief way this child attempted to communicate his story about a policeman directing traffic.

Another example is the following:

THE—MOSHNG—OR—DED

(8)

This particular child spent a long time making pictures each day during the writing period. He included a considerable amount of involved thought in this picture, whereas his words were extremely simple and short. In fact, this child, who progressed slowly in reading during his first-grade year, was still seeking reassurance about the actual process of putting words on paper at the end of the year. But he showed none of this self-doubt when drawing. His attempts to write without including pictures were frustrating for him, and he had much difficulty completing an assignment consisting of only writing.

At the second level, as children improved in reading and the writing process became more natural and comfortable, drawings did not receive as much attention. For some children, drawings still remained important, but words also became more important as a means of communication. The following example illustrates this growth. The picture is detailed, and shows motion and direction. This child was very concerned about the correctness of his drawing, made many erasures, and spent considerable time getting the picture just right. He had also done some research, selecting books on planes from the library.

A PSP-7 IS A HORS PAWRd PLAN, iT WeNT 1000 MIULS A AWR.

(9)

A story by another child shows that the picture continues to illustrate all the action in the words below it.

He lanDiD on the panit
He pot His fors feiDon He so A
PAthGoing to the casi He so GoDs
MAD of sceia ts With sunsor

(10)

This child read very well, and by the time he wrote this story, he was actively involved in his writing. He spent time planning what he wanted to write about; words at this point were as important to him as his pictures.

The third category was made up of children who had completely transferred the emphasis on pictures to an emphasis on text. The two samples here are from children reading on a first Primer level. By the time they had reached this reading level, they were no longer including pictures in their stories at all.

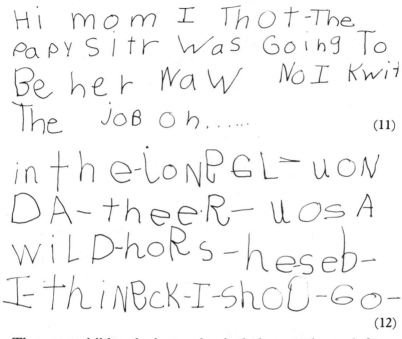

Hi mom I Thot The papy Sitr Was Going To Be her Naw No I Kwit The Job Oh..... (11)

in the LoNPGL~ uON DA-theeR- uos A WiLD-hoRs-heseb- I-thiNPck-I-shoD-Go- (12)

These two children had started to include quoted speech from people or animals, although they did not include quotation marks. It was appropriate therefore to introduce both children to their use at this time. They were obviously writing down their thoughts more completely than merely telling about what they drew. My observations would suggest that, as children finish their first grade year, the importance of written words increases.

Coping with Problems and Frustrations

Are there children who do not seem to be able to use this writing process? Yes! Anyone who works with children knows that of course there are exceptions. For me, two children come to mind. One is a child who had great difficulty with the phonetic approach to reading. She could not write down the correct letter for a sound she heard pronounced orally. She could tell me what the beginning and ending consonant sounds were in the word "puppy," but would write down a completely incorrect letter such as "d" for the "p" sound. Her writing consisted of random letters clustered in groups. It was impossible for me to translate, and she could not remember what she had tried to write down, even when I got to her almost immediately. After one and a half years of intensive remedial help in reading, she was finally able to read on a second Primer level. But she still had problems writing. For instance:

P brot mP dog it wus fun vay
had u owd DURY
Bafur   VEY   OR   CK Los TO
Now   HM sh R ....   (13)

She said that the words *owd DURY* represented "old path," and *BAFUR* meant "before," but she had trouble remembering what the words were supposed to be and had to try to recall what she meant to say. (Each time I review this example, I think she initially wrote "an old dirty bathroom.") However, the progress she had made in this year and a half was considerable. Her look of pleasure when I was able to read one of her stories without her aid was a delight to see. Even though it took her three times as long to reach a coherent product as it did most of the other children, her pride in a published book that I had been able to translate was just as great as any other child's. My message to teachers is: stick with it! A breakthrough will eventually happen.

Other children who have difficulty with the invented spelling process are those whose first language is not English. These children often write down letters representing sounds in their first learned language. However, by the time they become comfortable in speaking and reading English, these children have reached the same level of translatable writing as those whose first language is English. When an ESL child continues to have a great deal of difficulty it probably means there are other problems in the beginning reading process. For example, a Spanish-speaking child from Chile in second grade still could not easily decode phonetically and had no sight vocabulary. This excerpt is typical of his work:

a uan to mae   cash   datdae

which meant "I went to my cousin's birthday." His writing also improved as his reading ability increased through remediation.

Supporting the Process

Through this entire first year, the encouragement and support I received from the other teachers in the system who were also using the process approach were extremely valuable to me. We met regularly, shared our frustrations and doubts, discussed the "exceptions" we encountered, and received ideas from each other. The fact that I was not alone in my experiences added to my confidence in pursuing this approach to writing. Actual writing samples illustrated our successes and failures. The successes increased as that first year went on, and we were able to see such positive evidence from a number of classrooms, not just our own. Consequently, the substantial amount of good feeling from other adults and from the children helped to boost my own confidence in continuing to use the process approach to writing in my classroom.

Explaining the Process to Parents

Increasing confidence also gave me the courage to introduce and explain the new approach to parents. Naturally, I was very concerned about their possible reactions. School and their child's progress and achievement are trememdously important to them, and I was very uneasy presenting a process that did not first teach children to spell correctly. The idea of displaying work that included uncorrected spelling and imperfect handwriting was contrary to what I thought parents would want to see. During the first year, the class had completed a unit on career education, and I had collected all the follow-up written exercises the children had done and made "Job Books" out of them. Reluctant to send this work home without a cover letter explaining the writing process, I prepared one and clipped it to each book as it went home (a sample letter is included in the chapter "Explaining the Writing Process Approach to Parents"). Much to my surprise, not one parent came in to discuss anything. When talking with me in conferences and when chatting while they dropped off and picked up their children, they expressed only delight. Their children felt proud of their books, were comfortable with writing, and were writing spontaneously at home.

In subsequent years, I have talked extensively to parents about the process approach to writing in the classroom in the fall conference and during Open House Night in October. I have always made sure that concrete examples were present for viewing. That first published book and a child's pride and excitement about it seem to allay all suspicion and doubt. By the end of their child's first year, the parents are equally comfortable with this approach to writing.

In thinking about the process I have gone through in learning about this writing method, I am most impressed with its naturalness for small children. It builds on what children do themselves when left with crayons, pencils, paper, and felt pens. Instead of holding children back from producing valuable materials until they learn to read and spell, it encourages, approves of, and helps to implement children's interest in expressing their own creative and imaginative thoughts and ideas. The acceptance and praise teachers give to children at this early age for their actual writing leads them to self-acceptance. This self-acceptance paves the way for their growth in being able to revise, rethink, and improve their writing skills and abilities in future years. I am convinced of the value of this method of writing for children.

It works! It's fun! It brings results!

The message at the beginning of this chapter says: "On my vacation we went to my cousin's house." Did you decipher it?

Translations

1. My dog got puppies.
2. And I saw a lion. He asked me my name. (It) was Abby.
3. We went to Mars. When we got there we saw Martians.
4. This is a space ship.
5. The tigers (that) like to ride bikes. They have some bikes that they don't use.

6. There was a city that got blown up by an American plane. It was a German city.
7. Our Trip to California
   Once my sister had a friend.
   Her name is Laura Platt. We are
   going to visit her in February and
   we are also going to see our
   Nani and Grampa.
8. The Martians are dead.
9. A PSP-7 is a horsepower plane. It went 1,000 miles an hour.
10. He landed on the planet. He put his force field down. He saw a path going to the castle. He saw gods made of skeletons with a sensor.
11. "Hi, Mom. I thought the babysitter was going to be here now." "No, I quit the job on . . ."
12. In the jungle one day there was a wild horse. He said, "I think I should go . . ."
13. I brought my dog. It was fun. They had on old path. Before we were close to New Hampshire . . .

2. Becoming an Author: Second and Third Grade

Deborah D'Amico

Setting Up

More than anything else, success with a process approach to writing rests upon the teacher and her ability to suspend nearly all she has come to know and expect of children's writing. Even before the children begin to use this new approach, the teacher must have in place, both in the classroom and in her mind, a system for organizing herself and her children and a different orientation toward the task of writing. No longer will she want to send written work home as soon as the ink is dry. Nor will she be expecting a "finished copy" of one piece before another can be started. She will, instead, want to offer her children a system that will allow them to file, locate, rework and refile their stories. She will need to offer them several ways to tackle successfully the task of writing and will want at hand a variety of papers, pens and even recording equipment. And she will need time—time when she is free from other instructional responsibilities, time when all of the children are together, time that will, as nearly as possible, not be negotiable.

I was, by no means, able to meet all of these challenges in my first year of using a process approach to writing with my second and third graders. In fact, some of these problems and many more were not evident to me until we were well underway! In that first year, I learned a tremendous amount about writing, about children, and about myself as a teacher.

The careful filing of children's work is a surprisingly difficult problem to solve. I was amazed at the volume of written work some children could stockpile in a given month. My first idea was to give each child a large "file," which I made by folding an 18" × 24" piece of oak tag and writing the child's

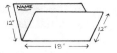

name on the top. I then filed these alphabetically by first name in a large storage bin with a divider for each letter. Into this file the children were told to place all of their writing: first drafts, finished pieces, ideas and drawings. As can be well imagined, in no time the files of most children became crammed full, and many pieces were being ripped or even misfiled in haste. This situation, coupled with my intention of keeping all of the children's writing from September to June, quickly made my filing system unworkable.

I decided to have the children separate their different pieces according to what "stage" they were in. The large file was maintained, but only for completed pieces. Works in progess, notes, ideas, and drawings were placed in individual folders given to each child to keep in his or her storage area. I found some ideal ones with pockets on the inside covers, left over from another class. When I explained to the children that many authors kept just such a notebook for unfinished work, ideas, or even lists, they were thrilled! Using these folders eliminated the daily rummaging through the alphabetical file which had proved so damaging to filed writing. The children could now begin their daily writing task by simply taking their folders to their work space and opening them up.

At the outset, I felt it was important to be consistent in scheduling writing. I wanted the children to know that writing was a clear priority in our room, and that all were expected to participate. I scheduled writing for thirty minutes each morning. With all my children busy writing at their desks, I felt free to pull some of them for reading instruction or a math lesson. A surprising number of weeks passed before I realized the inconsistency of such scheduling! On the one hand, I was setting aside a sizable chunk of class time for the children to write because I felt it was important. At the same time, I apparently took it lightly enough to pull some of them from it to do something else. And, to make matters even more confusing, I wasn't even available to the children as they wrote! Clearly a change was in order.

I moved writing time to the afternoon, a part of the day when I was free from instructional tasks, and scheduled it only three days per week instead of five. This is one of several areas where the teacher can adjust the program according to her particular schedule and the children's needs. For my classroom, it seemed unrealistic to plan that the children would write every day. I felt it was more important to offer my children three sessions per week of quality writing time than to try to squeeze in two more just to be able to say that the children wrote every day. The children had no trouble carrying their ideas over a day when they didn't write, and the writing folder really helped to keep them focused when they resumed writing on the following day. I also felt more relaxed and more connected with the children as writers. Now my availability allowed me to circulate and interact with the children as they wrote. Initially the writing period lasted twenty minutes. As the year progressed, I expanded it to thirty, and then to forty-five minutes.

Because of the age range in my classroom, it was important to have a variety of writing paper available for the children's use. In addition to the inexpensive lined yellow paper, I had supplies of larger-lined handwriting paper, and large story paper with a space at the top for drawing. When I realized that some children were overwhelmed by the large size of the story paper, I cut it in half and offered the children both sizes. Some inexpensive drawing paper was also needed for children to draw on before, during, and after working on a story. Crayons and skinny magic markers added color and detail to the pictures and, hence, to the stories as well. I also had a tape recorder and a supply of blank tapes available for helping reluctant writers get started, or prolific writers get focused.

Getting Started

Getting children started on a writing task is difficult, no matter what the approach. And asking children to draw from their personal experience for a writing topic can diminish even the most outgoing child's enthusiasm. Such nonfiction writing, however, was the thrust of my writing program. Despite the inherent difficulties, I am convinced that the children ultimately work better when nonfiction writing is the bulk of what they produce.

My children were used to writing programs that allowed them to write fiction any time they chose—and they nearly always chose to do so. My own plans for them would constitute a big change, and so, needed some justification. I began our first writing period something like this:

"This year, you'll be working like real authors to become better and better writers. You're lucky because you can learn a lot from authors. For example, did you know that most authors keep a folder of drawings, photographs, lists, names, or story beginnings just to help give them writing ideas? You'll be keeping a writing folder too, just for your own story ideas. Did you also know that authors share their unfinished stories with people they like and trust? That helps them get ideas about how to make their writing better. You'll be sharing your ideas and stories with each other and with me so your own writing will get better and better. Most important, and maybe the hardest of all, authors have learned that they can do their best writing when they write about things that they know and care a lot about—things that are true or that have really happened in their own lives. For most of the time this year, you'll be writing about things that really happen to you."

The point needing emphasis is that of using nonfiction writing with young children. During the course of this process approach, you will be expecting your children to rework their writing for focus, clarity, and detail. For a child to reach for more detail or greater clarity in a piece of writing that originated in his or her imagination means reaching for something intangible and indefinite because it never existed in any real space or time. For example, the fairy princess's coach could be orange, blue or invisible. The space ship could blow up the enemy ships or disappear into hyperspace. The bunny rabbits could eat oatmeal for breakfast or visit the foxes for brunch. I have witnessed true exasperation as children attempted to pin down such details. Many such pieces are abandoned out of sheer frustration. But there really was one picnic when Aunt Sue fell into the lake wearing her new tennis outfit and not her nightgown or prom dress. And Joe's best friend really did throw a football through the window when his mom was watching, not when she was at the market. Such incidents are manageable because their action and characters are real and their duration finite. When using nonfiction topics, a child can write, share the writing, rewrite to answer the questions of clarification, and really bring the piece to a close. It is interesting to note as a point of encouragement that later in the year, when my children did write fiction and then rework their stories into final drafts, they were unanimous in their feeling that revising fiction was much harder to do than revising nonfiction.

Starting off with a clear explanation of the writing they would do, such as the one above, gives the children a rationale for one of the main components of the process—nonfiction writing. Once this component is explained, however, your battle is not won. It can be overwhelming for a child to be expected to write about something that really happened in his or her life. Not only are the possibilities endless, providing too much choice, but to reveal oneself so openly in writing can be devastating to a young child. You will want to base your own decision on how to begin by assessing your children's strengths and needs.

I found it helpful for the children to break the choices down into clear categories. For example:

a. a memorable incident
b. a memorable person
c. a favorite pet
d. something you feel strongly about
e. a wish or hope for the future

It's important to note that the usual nonfiction topics such as "Last Weekend" are not what I mean here. Such a topic is too narrow. It takes from the children a choice that they can make more advantageously. Learning to narrow down a topic is one of the important steps in the process approach.

With the above list in mind, you might feel most comfortable choosing a topic yourself as the focus for the first writing session. By using, perhaps, one topic each week, you can provide your children with a choice that is workable, familiarize yourself and the children with the possibilities within each topic, and help the children relax with the idea of writing nonfiction.

Although choosing the broad topic for the children eliminates some of the headache, it also eliminates some of the fun! One of the most invigorating components of the process approach is helping the children generate writing ideas. Conducting a "sharing meeting," during which children discuss things that are on their minds—hence something important to them—is a fine way to generate topics and begin a writing period. Such activities are termed "warm-ups" and can take many forms, but always with the purpose of generating ideas and refocusing them into possible writing topics. In my class, we post an open agenda each week. Four children a day may sign up on the agenda to talk for five minutes each. They must indicate, on the agenda, what the focus of their talk will be. During such meetings each child takes charge of the time, relates the story, and then fields questions and comments from the class. I encourage children to listen to each other for writing ideas. Some children even bring their writing folders to agenda meetings to take notes, though the best results often come from plain, undistracted listening. After such meetings, while the topics are still fresh, we might brainstorm, as a class, a list of possible writing topics that might be taken from the meeting. Such lists might then be copied and filed into each child's writing folder. At other times, I group children into pairs and ask them to work together for ten to fifteen minutes to come up with possible writing ideas for each of them. By directing them to focus on what the agenda meeting made each of them think of in their own experience, such classroom sharing helps the topics become more personal.

Thinking of warm-ups can be one of the most enjoyable parts of the process approach. Don't be afraid to use your imagination. After a two-week winter vacation, my children returned full of stories about how they had spent their time. I wanted to offer them some way of focusing on the incidents which they found most memorable, and recording them in some unusual way, enabling them to draw on these as writing topics in the weeks ahead. I decided to have them make time lines which would order and display the most important parts of their vacations. Using words and pictures, the children spent an afternoon constructing individual time lines. Once completed and shared with the group, the time lines were displayed around the room. Each child could then go to his or her time line at writing time and choose one of the incidents illustrated as a writing topic. This was enormously successful and many children used these time lines for several weeks.

One day, at the beginning of writing time, I told the children that we were going to build a web to help us warm up for writing. I then put the word PET on the board. I asked the children to tell me what word or words came into their minds when they saw the word PET . As the children volunteered their ideas, I wrote them and connected them to the original word. The web looked something like this:

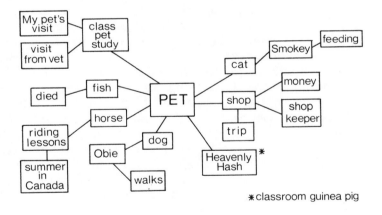

*classroom guinea pig

As the web grew, so did the variety of responses and the enthusiasm of the class. When we finished we talked briefly about some of the ideas we'd generated, and then the children went off to work on focusing their own ideas about pets.

It's important to note that, at the end of such warm-ups, the children were not required to use any of the ideas. In fact, once my writing program was underway, the children were often at different stages of the writing process: some continuing a story started two days previously, others working on a new idea, still others conferencing, revising, rewriting, or illustrating. Warm-ups helped those already working on a story to compile fresh ideas to tuck away in their writing folders for possible use later. Those children who were stuck for an idea, or who needed to put aside something that wasn't going well and start something fresh, used the warm-ups as an immediate source of new ideas.

Writing

Many different stages are necessary to good writing, not all of which include putting pencil to paper! In using a process approach to writing, you will need to become comfortable with some unconventional means toward the end of writing. Children must be able to move around, and to talk freely with each other or with the teacher. They need to be able to draw, to dictate, or to copy. They must be allowed to experiment with spelling, to cut apart their stories, mark them up with arrows, stars or circles, or abandon a story that has become frustrating or uninteresting. Writing period, then, is an active but productively busy time during which children and teacher are involved in any one of a series of tasks. In short, actual writing may not always be the end product of a writing period for every child!

The main goal in writing for second and third graders is almost always to establish a clear, workable focus. Even after they have chosen a topic, actually getting started remains a hurdle for many children. At this point, conversation may be the best remedy. By talking an idea through, children can be helped to realize that they know more about how to begin than they think. Ruth, for example, was having trouble getting started one day. Our conversation follows:

R: I don't know what to write down.
T: You've chosen a topic?
R: Yes, I'm going to write about our trip to New Hampshire, but I don't know how to start.

T: Why don't you tell me a little bit about your trip.

R: Well, it was fun. We went to my cousin's in Derry. They live on a farm with cows and pigs. They used to have four horses but they sold two of them last year. They have a garden and they grow hay in their field for their cows. They milk them and sell the milk to a dairy.

T: It sounds like a great farm. I can get a really good picture in my mind of it. Would you like to write a description of the farm or write about your trip to visit it?

R: I think I'll describe it this time and then maybe use the trip as a topic another day.

T: Great! Be sure to make a note of that in your writing folder.

Conversation among students can be just as helpful. Here is one between Freddy, who was having trouble getting started, and two friends, Bill and Jerry, who were each working on a story.

Freddy: I don't know what to write.

Jerry: You could write about seeing "Superman II."

Freddy: No, I don't want to. That's boring.

Bill: You should see my brother, he's so weird! Last night he was running around the house pretending to be Superman. He kept yelling "Supermaaaaan! Supermaaaaan!" My mother was getting sick of it!

Freddy: (Laughing.) Oh yeah, my brother is weird too! Once he was going to pretend to be spiderman. So he got up onto the bureau and jumped off! We were upstairs and he made a huge crash when he landed.

Jerry: Was anyone else home?

Freddy: (Grinning—really animated now.) Oh yes! My mother came upstairs all worried that someone had been hurt. When she found out that it was just Greg fooling around she really got mad!!

Bill: Hey, you could use that as a writing topic! It's pretty funny.

Freddy: Yeah, I could. (He chuckles to himself as he begins to write.)

In each case, being allowed to converse freely during writing period was essential to each child's eventual start at the writing task. Often such conversations went on a lot longer, sometimes lasting the entire writing period. Initially, I found it difficult to relax with such a use of writing time, and found myself cutting such conversation short with a reminder to "get busy." One day, however, I decided to let a group of children continue their conversation until five minutes before the period was over. I then approached them and said that I'd noticed that they'd been talking almost all period. They looked pretty sheepish so I quickly added that authors often find such conversations really helpful to them because they get lots of topic ideas from them. I then directed them to use the remaining five minutes to list every thing they'd talked about. When they'd finished their list, whose length surprised them, I asked them to make copies for each to place in his writing folder for later use. By making this clear link between relaxed conversation and the writing process, I wanted the children to see that writing really does come out of their own experiences.

Be ready for the child who does *nothing* day after day during writing period! He stares at the wall, sharpens his unused pencil, gets his snack (in three trips to the coatroom) and, when asked, says, "I'm thinking, but I don't know what to write about." There's one in every crowd—guaranteed! Mine was Matt. Even conversations with peers didn't help because such interactions usually degenerated quickly into horsing around. Finally, pen and pencil in hand, and at my wit's end, I pulled a chair up next to Matt's workspace:

T: OK, Matt, we're going to make a list of all the things you could possibly write about.

M: But there *is* nothing! There never is!

T: OK, let's make that the first one! (writing) I'll bet we can get ten on this list in the next two minutes. What else? Didn't you talk about something today at agenda meeting?

M: My new bike.

T: That's number two! That would be interesting to hear about. (Two or three children have wandered over, curious about what's going on. They chime in.)

1: What about your trip to Barbados, Matt!

T: Good! That's three! We're on our way!

M: I got new sneakers Saturday.

T: Number four!

2: Have you seen any movies lately?

M: I went to "Raiders of the Lost Ark." It was great! (I write it down.) I could write about bubble gum.

T: (writing) Bubble gum?? What do you mean?

M: I love to chew it, but my mom won't let me so I sneak it when she's not around!

T: That sounds like a very interesting topic, Matt. Only four more ideas to get ten!

M: (really enthusiastic now) I'll bet we can get more than ten!

We wound up with about fifteen topics for Matt, which he placed in his writing folder. He ended that period by writing about bubble gum, and he went back to that list for the remainder of the year whenever he got stuck.

This method of getting started is fairly structured, but necessary for those children who are always overwhelmed by the choice and need a list of possible topics to fall back on. Don't be afraid to resort to such tactics for children who are truly stuck.

Picture drawing can be useful at many stages of the process. Several of my children began expressing each new idea by drawing a picture. Their writing initially described the picture. Eventually, with encouragement, the children expanded their thoughts to include greater detail. The picture then served as a kind of cementing of the original idea.

This is an autograph from Tom Feelings.
I got it in the auditorium.

At other times, pictures can help focus an otherwise rambling story. When bogged down in the middle of a piece of writing, my children often found it helpful to illustrate what they thought was the most interesting part of their story. Once completed, the picture helped to refocus the author, who could revise or begin the story again accordingly.

The tape recorder is one of the most popular tools during writing period. I was able to supply one tape for every two children, clearly marked with each child's name and carefully stored for use during writing. The tapes were used, again, at various stages of the process. Children found it helpful to talk their writing ideas onto the tape before beginning to write. Others would read and then listen to their first drafts. Hearing his or her own voice and ideas on tape removed the author from the writing just enough to gain a more objective view of the work thus far. A rambling story was quickly revealed as such when the writer had to listen to it! The most interesting parts of a dull story became clear. It's a method worth trying.

As can be seen, each of the strategies mentioned helped toward the goals of establishing a focus and getting started. Taping, listing, drawing, talking—all are fairly unorthodox activities when included under the heading of writing. But when you consider that starting with a clear focus is one of the most difficult, yet most important writing tasks, even for adult authors, such methods become easily justifiable when the authors are so young.

My role as teacher was also unusual but, for that reason, refreshing and fun! It was important that I be available during writing. This meant that I circulated among the children, clipboard and pen in hand, encouraging, listening, reacting, refocusing, and checking in with each child on his or her piece of writing. I found it helpful to use a record sheet that kept track of what each child was doing during each writing period (a sample follows). Using this grid, I was able to jot down quick notes, for myself and the child, and see progress over a series of days and weeks. It also helped to make clear whose writing was at a standstill or which child I was not checking on as the days went by.

As the year progressed, the children began to love the writing period. Their enjoyment fed my own enthusiasm which, in turn, encouraged them to think of themselves more and more as real authors with something worthwhile to say. They began to take great pride in the fact that their writing skills were improving noticeably. Most children quickly moved from being shy and unsure with their ideas to being confident and willing to share what they were doing with others. This confidence and willingness led us naturally into a new phase of the process: conferencing.

	12/4	12/7	1/6	1/8	1/11	1/13	1/22
ANN	xmas note		raccoon in yard →	* very good	Jaimie's B-day (lots of run-ons) →	run-ons corrected	abs.
AUDRY			christmas	No time			Dentist trip
JOE	* Mom's Baby		going to see Cinderella →	no time	Cinderella story		
DONNA	A play called Nancy Potato		christmas →		sister's Birthday		new pants
JULIA	Design blocks poem		concert at symphony →	very good job *			
JERRY			Bill's Birthday party →	no time	Bill's Birthday	read to me, corrected spelling →	
RUTH	Xmas note		baby cousin 6 mo. old →	fantastic story * clean concise	visit with cousins		ants for farm
CHARLIE	Barbarians		stomper →				
MATT	poked in the eye	pizza on day eye poked	fish observation	Charley's friendship →		Abs.	
DWAYNE	fish observation		Best Thing about vacation			raccoon story	

Conferencing

There is great potential for instant success with conferencing! In general, children are itching to read their writing to someone whose opinion they value: their teacher or a friend. Our job, as teachers, is to make that enthusiasm work for us by channelling it into good conferencing techniques.

A conference can take many forms and, loosely defined, happens any time a child discusses his or her writing with someone else, and gets a reaction from the listener. As is true with most things that work well with children, the four conferencing styles which we used in my classroom evolved as responses to the children's needs. Through individual (teacher-child), whole-group (teacher-class), small-group (teacher-several children), and peer conferences (children on their own) the children began to develop a repertoire of ways to react to and help improve each other's writing. By listening critically to each other's stories, the children began to develop a clearer sense of the essence of writing, which helped them when they returned to their own work.

Conferencing in my classroom began in small steps. Early in the year, we discussed the fact that writers usually write for an audience, and that, because of this, they must attend to such things as focus, clarity and the development of an interesting topic or style so that people will want to read what they've written. I explained that we were going to help each other with this by listening to each other's writing. Then, during writing period, I listened. Sometimes I asked a child to read to me. More often I listened and reacted to a growing number of eager volunteers. It wasn't long before even the most reluctant author was sharing his or her work with me in these individual conferences.

The structure of such conferences grew naturally out of the needs that most of my second and third graders shared. As I have mentioned, focusing and starting to write were major hurdles. Once these had been overcome, however, the children's work had just begun. Maintaining that focus without a lot of extraneous information was very difficult for my young authors. Without assistance, they easily went off on tangents that had little to do with the focus of the writing. Some children could easily go on and on filling pages with irrelevant description and unnecessary detail. Thus I found myself trying out conferencing strategies that would help the children maintain and develop their focus with care.

One individual conference technique that helped was to ask a child to talk about his or her piece before he or she read it aloud. I discovered that even the most rambling writer could usually state the focus in one or two sentences:

> "Well, I'm writing about when I fell in the park and cut my head."

> "This is about my trip to New Hampshire to visit my cousins."

After such preliminary statements, it seemed logical to tell the child that that is what I would listen for as the piece was read. The conference thus assumed a structure of which both the author and the listener were aware. Often, after reading a piece of writing aloud at such times, the author was able to evaluate his or her own work:

> "I think I don't need to talk about what I ate for supper before going to the park."

> "My cousin loves to joke around so I want to leave that part in."

Often a child's piece contained many possible events on which he or she might focus. It was helpful with such pieces to ask the author what his or her favorite part was, assuming that the best writing is done with a topic the writer finds most compelling. For example, Bill wrote for six pages about the stock car races in New Hamsphire. His writing was interesting and descriptive, but too long to be workable because it included detail from the time he left home in the morning to the moment he went to bed! Here is an excerpt:

> Sunday afternoon I went to Seaconk Speedway. The pro stocks raced first. The charger division didn't race. Bugs won the modified races. There was an accident. Johnny flipped over. Reggie was on the top. Johnny took a trip upside down. Bugs just missed it. I went crazy! I wouldn't stop eating! My flag fell under the bleachers and some kids gave it back. Me and my cousin were freezing! I poured my drink out underneath the bleachers. I almost poured it on somebody's head. He started

to climb up the bleachers so I stepped on his fingers. Then two big kids got after me. My cousin said: "Don't worry, I'm here!" Then I had to go to the bathroom. We had to walk about a quarter of the track to get to the bathroom. After I went to the bathroom we ran all the way from the bathroom to the bleachers. The pro stocks were testing their fury. I think the Charger division is very loud. The Modifieds go fast. Me and my cousin were having an argument over who was going to win.

When I asked him what his favorite part was, Bill immediately focused on the incident during the race when he poured his drink down between the bleachers and onto someone's head! He wound up lifting that one incident out and writing about just that:

As you all know, I love car races. They're very boring at first, but then you get used to them. One time when I was at a race I poured my drink out underneath the bleachers. I almost poured it on somebody's head. He started to climb up the bleachers so I stepped on his fingers. Then two big kids got after me. My cousin said: "Don't worry, I'm here." Then I said: "That's what I'm worrying about." When the big kids reached us, my cousin was ready to fight it out with them. Lucky for us, just at that moment there was a big accident on the speedway. We all turned to watch and the big kids ran down the bleachers to be closer to the track. That was a close call!

Sometimes a child would approach me and say, "My story is stuck!" The author may have been working on it for several sessions, but now be losing momentum. He may no longer clearly remember the focus or find the topic exciting. In such situations, before I listened to the piece I asked the author what he or she thought was wrong with it. Asking a child to articulate exactly what's bothersome about the piece often helped to move him or her out of the slump. One such conversation went like this:

Ch: This story is boring.
  T: What's boring about it?

Ch: I don't know. It's just dumb. All I'm doing is listing the people at my birthday party.

 T: Was your party boring?

Ch: No.

 T: What made it fun?

Ch: We played some neat games and ate lots of food.

 T: Do you talk about the games in your story?

Ch: I'm going to, but I still am writing who was there.

 T: Can you think of some other way to write about your party? If this writing is boring, maybe it needs a little excitment added to it. How might you do that?

Ch: I don't know . . . maybe I could write about something fun that happened . . .

Individual conferencing became an important part of our writing period. I was confident about several approaches I could take to help the children improve their writing. Now I wanted the children to gain that same confidence in themselves and each other. I began to insist that they read their work to each other before they came to me. Most of the children took to this idea immediately and it was delightful to see a child hop up from his seat and take his writing to a friend to be shared, prefaced by a grinning "Listen to this!" Children took great pride in being chosen as a listener, and the whole idea of peer conferencing took off.

But having the children listen to each other was merely the first step. The next was to carry over into the peer conferences the structure that would allow the children to really help each other improve their writing. I was learning helpful conference techniques and needed an area in which I could model these for the children. Thus, the whole-group conference came about.

To set up a whole-group conference, I asked, at the beginning of writing period, for children to bring to the group a piece of their writing that they would like to read aloud. With each volunteer, I would then model some conferencing strategies that I had found useful in helping authors with their work. I behaved exactly as I had in individual conferences, asking the same questions: what are you writing about? what is your favorite part? what can we help you with? As the class observed over time, I reminded them that these were strategies that they could use when listening to someone's piece. Before long, I asked volunteers from within the group to comment on the piece just read and try to be helpful to the author. During these conference times, I kept notes of suggestions made to each author. The children took criticism from each other remarkably well, and they began to realize that they really did know what to listen for in a piece of writing. Toward the middle of the year at one such session, Matt, my most reluctant writer, surprised us by volunteering to read his writing. The interchange follows:

> M: (Holding up a drawing of water with a tiny dot in the middle and an arrow pointing to the dot.) I'm really not finished, but this is my drawing. My story says: "This is Barbados. I am going to it." I don't know what else to write.

> Ch 1: What's Barbados?
> M: It's an island that me and my mom are going to.
> Ch #2: How long are you going to be there?
> M: Fourteen days, I think.
> Ch #3: How will you get there?
> M: By plane.
> Ch 4: Why are you going?
> M: My mom is going to study about the children of Barbados, but I'm going to play.

I recorded the questions for Matt as they were asked. At the end of four or five minutes it was possible to point out to Matt that he really did know a lot more that could be added to his writing to make it longer and more interesting. When the children went off to write for the remainder of the period, I gave Matt the list of questions about his writing and asked him to see how many he could answer. Thus he was off and able to produce more material with which he could work.

The small group conference became my favorite because the interchange among the participants was always enthusiastic and the interest they displayed in each other's work sincere.

It began by chance. Bill had brought me yet another rambling account of one of his escapades. Again, he had produced five or six pages of writing that held at least three of four good topic possibilities. But one was, to my mind, a stand-out as the absolute best choice for his focus, and I was curious to see if other children would pinpoint the same one. After listening to Bill read, I asked him if he minded if some of the class listened to his writing. He didn't mind—in fact he seemed pleased—and I turned to the class, working busily at their own writing, and said, "Would some of you volunteer to come listen with me to what Bill's written?" Instantly we had four eager listeners. Bill's story read as follows:

> Saturday was my 9th birthday. It was a lot of fun. Jerry, Saul, Robbie and Karl came. Karl screwed up my party! He made a fool of himself. Karl was the dunce of the party. We had pizza for dinner. Philip was going to come but he didn't buy me a present. So he said: "he had company" but he really didn't have company. Tom didn't come either. I wish Tom and Philip came. It would have been funner with Tom and Philip. I like my watch the best. My watch has a stop watch. My party was pretty good. Even though it turned into a madhouse. We had cake a little while after dinner. The cake was very good. Jerry likes my brother's criss cross crash. Jerry gave me Bumbling Boxing . . .

When Bill finished reading I asked the listeners what one part they would like to hear more about. The unanimous response was the part about Karl messing up the party, which was exactly the part that I'd chosen myself. I told the children that I was excited because I felt that they were becoming very good listeners for each other, that they were learning a lot about what makes one topic more interesting than another. The listeners returned to their work justly pleased with themselves, and Bill went off to write about Karl's escapades at his party. Here is his second draft:

> Saturday was my 9th birthday. It was a lot of fun. Karl screwed up my party! He made a fool of himself. He took my new LeCube and threw it up in the air. He turned the party into a madhouse. He drove me nuts. I told him to cut it out! But my mother kept saying, "Bill, he's your guest." So I had to put up with it until he left.

I found peer conferences to be the most difficult type of conference to get used to because it was the type over which I had the least control. By definition, the teacher is not involved in a peer conference. When two children got together to discuss their writing, I was never sure what transpired! I needed to trust the children to be really purposeful and helpful to each other, but I also needed to be sure that they had command on some useful conferencing techniques which they could or would use in my absence. I tried several approaches. One was to give each child a list of the questions we had been using in whole-group, individual, and small-group conferences. Although some teachers in my school system had drawn up a very long list of questions, I wanted the children to generate their own by actually using them together, and observing their effects. Thus, our list grew as the year progressed, but began as follows:

> What can I do to be helpful to you?
> What can I listen for?
> What is your favorite part of this story?
> What are you writing about?
> How were you feeling when this was happening to you? Are your feelings clear in your writing?

In addition, I helped the children articulate exactly what some of their common problems had been as they wrote. Because they had all been involved in the process for a while, they easily came up with several difficulties that they might be able to help someone else through:

> Is there one clear focus to this story?
> Is this an interesting topic?
> Do things happen in order?
> Is there too much information here?

These criteria, along with the list of questions, were filed in each child's writing folder to be used during peer conferences.

Clearly then, conferencing can be used to improve the content of a piece of writing. Occasionally I was able to structure both individual and peer conferences to check on the mechanics of spelling, punctuation and grammar as well. In such cases, I chose as a helper a child who had struggled with the same issue confronting the author needing help. This was tremendously reinforcing all around. It helped the author with his or her writing and set up a situation in which he or she could learn from a peer. It also heightened the helper's self-confidence in an area that had been difficult, exposing him or her to that area one more time—a kind of instant review!

For example, Ann, who had had tremendous difficulty with run-on sentences, became a willing teacher for others once she had conquered the problem. Ruth's spelling was consistently careless and difficult for her to correct in her own work. However, she was able to help others find their own mistakes. Bill became a master at picking out topics from other's writing as well as his own.

Each type of conference continued to occur in my classroom throughout the year. The more the children listened to each other, the better they understood what good writing was. This growing understanding helped each child as he or she returned to his or her own work.

Drafting, Revising, Publishing

One of the tenets of the writing process approach is that the child, as writer, "owns" the piece of writing and, therefore, has final say as to when work on it stops. How do you know, then, when a piece is *really* finished? This was one of the most difficult questions to answer, because "finished" came to mean different things for different students at different times during the year. And if the teacher relinquishes "ownership" to the writer, how can she insist that a child work harder to reach for higher quality in his or her work? There were no easy answers for me, but I did come to some workable conclusions.

First, I had to accept that most of my children would *not* reach a definitive refinement of their writing abilities by the time they left my class. I had to see my work with them as one step in the long process of developing them as writers. It also helped me to remember what it was I hoped to see in my second and third graders' writing: a focus and a clarity of style that made the writing interesting. Clearly each child would be at a different stage of development toward these goals and would need different encouragement to help him or her along. Thus the difference in the definition of when a piece is "done."

Because the process involved in finishing a first draft was the thrust of my program, many pieces never went beyond that stage. When you consider the quality of thinking that goes into deciding on a topic, narrowing it down to a manageable focus, beginning to write, conferencing to re-sort ideas and details, and finishing the piece, it is easier to understand why a completed first draft can be regarded as an end point. Ownership came into play when a draft was finished, and the writer had had a conference with me to discuss how the piece had taken shape and what alterations, if any, might be made. At such times, when I asked a child, "What would you like to do with this now?" I was really willing to let him or her decide. There were several possibilities from which the child might choose: writing another draft to include the changes, working through that second—or maybe third or fourth—draft to "publication," or simply filing this first draft away, with any suggestions written on it, possibly to be attacked fresh at a later date. The motivation to "publish," that is, to make a final revised, edited, and illustrated copy to go into the class library, was great enough to spur most children on beyond one draft. Many children also chose to return to a first draft later in the year, so this was seldom a stage where work really did stop. It became a question of trusting the value of the process and recognizing that a final, neat, finished product was no longer the main goal.

I did encounter children who needed more structure and clearer goals in order to move ahead in their skills as writers. Careful record-keeping enabled me to keep track of when I had last had a conference with them, how many pieces they had brought through a first draft stage, and even how they had spent the writing time over several days. Clear choices were also necessary. Brainstorming an individual list of possible story ideas and setting a time limit on when a first draft was expected were strategies I did not always rigidly employ, but which were certainly appropriate for some children.

Grammar, Spelling, Mechanics

As the year unfolded, I began to recognize many opportunities within the writing program to reinforce such skills as punctuation, capitalization, and spelling. The first and most obvious was to bring together a small group of children who seemed to be having the same difficulty and, using their own writing, strengthen their skills. For example, proper capitalization was particularly difficult for some second graders. By working together with each other's writing, they understood the importance of mastering the skill and they realized how communication is affected by improper use of capitals. Spelling errors were corrected in much the same way. Children can often spot misspelled words in someone else's work more quickly than in their own. Working in a small group correcting each other's work helped some of my children enormously.

Sometimes I used an individual conference to work with a child on a particular problem he or she was having. Ann's stories were always one continuous sentence from start to finish:

> On my sister's birthday at 2:00 my father came home and we had the birthday party and we had the cake and my sister didn't want to open her presents and me and my brother opened her presents and she got a little dog and a cooking set and money and a Miss Piggy car and the cake tasted good. . . .

I worked with Ann in stages, first having her underline all of the "ands" in her piece. Then, together, we decided which ones were necessary and which could go. After only a few such exercises, in which Ann was given increasing responsibility for each step in the process, she seemed to grasp the concept. One day she spontaneously presented me with an old draft she had retrieved from her writer's folder. She grinned broadly and said, "Debbie, look at what I did!" She had gone through the piece, first underlining all the "ands" and then eliminating those she felt weren't needed! It was exciting to see that she really could apply the skill she had mastered and that she did so voluntarily!

The gratification that such learning presented to me and to the children cannot be emphasized too much. One of the most exciting aspects of the process approach was that evidence of such understanding about writing really did occur with increasing frequency as the year progressed. When Bill decided to lift the part of his racing car episode he wished to focus on as a new topic, he literally lifted it—he cut it out of the old piece and taped it to a new piece of paper, explaining to me as he did so: "I'm going to tape this in the middle of the page because I want to write something before and after it." A lesson in leads and appropriate story sequence couldn't have cemented this notion in his mind any more clearly. When Ruth crossed out a phrase because, in her words, "it makes the story too romantic," I was amazed at the sense of tone and style she had developed by reading and reworking her own writing, and by listening and reacting to the writing of others.

A writing program that includes a lot of discussion reinforces the use of proper grammar and sentence structure. Over time, the change in my children's work became evident. With careful planning, a teacher can introduce spelling skills within the program, making a more structured spelling program, with weekly lists and tests, unnecessary.

The possibilities for using the children's own writing as the basis for such learning are virtually endless. Children grasp concepts much more quickly and firmly when the material they are considering is something they have created themselves.

Summary

Using a process approach to teach writing is not the easy way out. On the contrary, it is time-consuming because it is so highly individualized and demands your full attention and energy during the writing period. It is different enough from what you, your children, and their parents are likely to be used to that it needs a lot of justification and explanation. The goals must be clear enough in your mind, and the steps of the process clear enough to your children that even slight progress can be measured over time. You, as the teacher, have to be willing to let go of many of your assumptions about how children learn to write.

Despite all of this, I am hooked! After a year of struggling to get underway and grappling with the road blocks as they arose, I would not go back to my old methods for any reason. The excitement my children felt about their writing was genuine, the pride they took in their accomplishments was justified. By midyear, writing period was the favorite time of day for many of my children. Even the requirement to do nonfiction writing was no longer distasteful to them. In fact, when given the choice of fiction or nonfiction, most children chose nonfiction because they felt it was easier to revise.

I am sure that my children left my classroom in June more

confident writers and with a firmer sense of what good writing entails. They were very aware of how much they had learned and realized that it had come about, chiefly, through their own hard work. How encouraging when what we do as teachers produces such solid and rewarding results.

3. Expanding Ideas: Fourth Grade

Ilene Salo-Miller

Getting Started

Getting children involved in thinking about writing can be a difficult task, but it can be made easier if children have an active role in the procedure. I use many different approaches to get children excited about writing. One approach is the morning sharing time when we all listen to each other's stories.

I gather everyone in a circle and have them talk about their "unforgettable" time at the toy store, or at a baseball game, or just let them recount silly times with their pals. I become an active listener, anxious to hear the next part of their tales! When children hear their peers talking about their experiences, it triggers their own ideas, which slowly weave themselves into unique story starters. I always try to give everyone a chance to entertain us with an experience they've lived through, and the children and I often interrupt the teller to ask questions about what happened so that everyone feels a sense of *really* being listened to. I like to watch my class laugh at and relate to each others' experiences. No one is ever forced to share an experience or a piece of writing if he or she chooses not to. I have found that after a while, even the shy children will feel comfortable enough to share.

I pass out a prewriting sheet to the class after they've talked, and they fill it in. This lets them continue thinking along the same lines as the group discussion. The sheet looks like this:

Prewriting Ideas

1. Unforgettable or interesting experiences.

2. Sad or happy memories.

3. Important people in my life.

4. Embarrassing moments I've had or shared with a friend.

5. Fun times with pets.

6. Other subjects I may want to write about.

I leave spaces between each idea so the children can fill in the sheet with phrases or sentences that will help them recall information for their first story. When they start their first piece of writing, they use an idea from this prewriting activity sheet.

I let the students work in small groups as they write so they can talk to each other and continue to get ideas from each other. This keeps the enthusiasm high. If someone is having difficulty beginning, I spend some time alone with that child asking questions and suggesting ideas.

I find that the children can write more freely and accurately when they begin with a true story. In this way they have information that is real to them to rely on when they write. Children easily remember a unique experience they have had with a family member or a friend. I try to start there. If they can't remember one, I call on another child who is busy writing to share what he or she has written so far. Often this provides an example of what is expected and gets the slow starter off the mark. I always make it a point to visit the children, individually, as they begin, and show real interest in their topics. I point out the positive parts of the children's stories to keep them writing, even though I know they need to work on what they've written. Most children accept criticism better after they have been told that they have the makings of a great story! My exuberance gives my children all the more initiative to write because they know I'll be right there encouraging them. I also know that beginning to write can be a difficult task for some children. I try to reduce anxiety before it overcomes the child.

Another method I've had success with involves drawing. If I notice that children are not able to start and are becoming frustrated, I have them draw a scene from an experience they remember. The children who are slow starters usually jump at the opportunity to draw! After I see a picture developing, I have a conference with the artist and ask him or her questions about it. I might ask, "Oh, where were you when you saw this huge dog you just drew?" or "What was the dog barking at?" or "Why didn't the dog have anyone holding its leash?" With questions of this kind I can get a feeling for what this child is attempting to say. After I get some specific answers, I tell the child that this scene would make a terrific *written* story, and since he already has drawn a picture of it, why not write it out?

What if a child doesn't want to draw or write? Then I try a tape recorder. Some of my children feel much more comfortable talking out their stories from beginning to end. I make it clear to them that if they use the recorder, a written product has to follow.

Once my class begins to write, I like to stress the idea that beginning sentences get readers quickly involved in their stories. I do this by talking about and demonstrating "leads." Then I have the children write three different leads for their stories. I stress that each lead should grab the reader's interest, that the children should get more specific and exciting as they state the same idea, and that good leads help the writers get off to a good start.

Lead 1: The other day I went on a plane ride.
Lead 2: Whoops! The plane lifted off with a jolt.

These two examples show progress because they help readers form pictures in their minds. Lead 2 is obviously more exciting and specific—that's what the goal of this exercise is.

I always seek examples of good leads in the books the children are reading, or in a book that I may be reading aloud to them. The more examples the children see and hear, the greater their chance for success when they write their own leads. I make it a point to ask the children which lead gives them a better picture of what's happening in the story.

Here is a typical example of progression from a dull beginning to one with some vitality:

1. One day I got out of bed.
2. One bright morning I got out of my warm bed.
3. One bright, cold morning, the smoke alarm went off and I stumbled out of my warm bed. Smoke was creeping under my door.

The leads should get more specific and be aimed very precisely at the point of the story. The children may discuss their sentences with a friend once they have finished all three leads so that they get some feedback on which lead is best.

One of the children came to me once and said, "Sara likes my first lead, but I really think my third lead is better—which should I choose?" I solved this dilemma by saying, "Well, Patricia, you're the author and authors at times have tough decisions to make! Remember, you own the story and you have to do what you think is best!" By continually emphasizing that the children are the owners and authors of their own work, the class gets a feeling for the responsibility that goes along with being a writer. As the children continue to write, I go around and ask how their stories are coming along. They are very eager to begin sharing what they are writing or thinking. Such sharing is a very important part of the process approach, and a step in the direction of conferencing. Some of my children will ask me to listen to what they have just written, or I'll hear, "Oh, listen to what I'm going to say about my little brother's bad habits." I make it a point to have a brief fifteen to twenty second chat to keep the ideas flowing. Most children enjoy the chance to talk with a teacher or other students.

This interaction is extremely important in all aspects of the process approach to writing. As the children approach me and I begin to read or hear about their adventures, I try to tune into a specific, unclear portion of their story in order to ask a probing question or two that might help clarify or add details to what they have written.

After I have walked around a few times and peeked into the beginnings of some stories, I try to generate more interest in leads. I try to spot a creative first sentence and immediately say "Listen to this beginning that John has just written. Doesn't it make you want to find out more about what happened? Keep writing, John—we can hardly wait for more!" This generally keeps the children's enthusiasm high, and often they will want me to share what they've written with the class. I really find that the more I involve everyone, the better results I get.

After the children have been writing and talking for a while, I often hear the famous last words, "OK, Mrs. Miller, I'm all finished with my story—here it is!" In the past, I would have said "Fine, let me correct your spelling and sentence structure, and you can rewrite it neatly." But in using the process approach to writing, I soon discovered that when I was presented with this first draft, my work and my children's work were just beginning! Teaching children that writing is a process made up of many steps is not an easy task, but I found that when I explained to them about an author's responsibility to his or her readers to produce his best story possible, their enthusiasm remained fairly high.

Conferencing in its many different forms is a great way to teach children to listen to their own story and each other's, to expand on their ideas, and to rework or revise what they've written. Through conferencing, the children become more adept at improving their written work.

I introduce the concept of conferencing with a whole-group approach. I start with one child's written story. The child and I sit in front of the rest of the class and I have the child read his or her story out loud, slowly and clearly. When the child finishes, I encourage compliments or positive comments *only*. We will deal with problems in the story later. The child now has a positive feeling about what he or she has written and can accept help more readily. After I've called on some of the children who want to comment, I begin to ask some questions myself to help the authors think of ways to expand or clarify their stories. Later, the children use these questions for their own conferencing time. Below is a sample of a conference sheet with the questions I ask.

Conference Sheet

Remember to say something positive about the story you have just read.

1. Does the story have a *title*? If not, try to think of one.
2. Is the *lead* interesting? Does it make you want to read on? If not, try to improve on it.

3. Ask the author what his or her favorite *part* of the story is. Is it explained in detail so you, the reader, can really picture what's going on? If not, try to help the author expand it. Ask the author questions.
4. Has the author done a good and detailed job of describing *characters* in his or her story? If not, try to help the author describe the characters so you can see them.
5. Has the author kept to one story or *plot* or does the story have too many stories in it? What can you and the author do to help stick to one plot?
6. Does the story have an *ending* or does the author leave his readers dangling?
7. Does the story have a *setting*? Can you picture where the story takes place?
8. Ask the author what his/her least favorite part of the story is. Is it necessary to have this part, or what can you both do to help make it more interesting or exciting to the reader.
9. Is there anything about the story that you can't quite seem to understand? *Ask the author questions* and try to get him/her to explain in detail the parts that are unclear. *How* and *why* questions are valuable and lead to explanations and answers. Remember: the author's own their stories and have the final choice of what they want to *revise* or edit.

Good luck authors

This is just a sample of some of the questions that have worked for my children when they are conferencing. When I am having my whole-group conference, I go over each of these questions and review and stress the important concepts, such as setting, character development, plot, and lead. I really use this group time to role-play a conference, and I find that the more dramatic I am, the more the children tune in and begin to develop a "knack" for the conferencing process. I make it a point to try to have the author explain any parts that I find hard to understand. Thus, the verbal part of revision has begun. As I ask more questions from the conference sheet, I am also recording on a piece of paper some of the revisions or additions that the author has agreed to make, so that at the end of our conference, I can hand the child the sheet and he or she will know what needs work. I try to do one whole-group conference a day for about a week just to assure myself that the class is getting a feeling for what goes into a conference.

With practice, they get to know what to look for in their writing.

When I feel that the children have a handle on how to go about having a conference, I give them the chance to conference "formally" with a friend. From the start, they've always had the opportunity to talk about and read their stories to me or to the class, but now is the time for them to sit down with each other or with me and concentrate on revising.

The children bring their writing folders to the conference. Each child in the class has a writing folder with pockets in which he or she keeps all written work. This is a good way for the children and me to feel more organized, and to avoid the frustration of having papers all over the room. The children begin their peer conferencing by finding a partner. I tell the children to find an out-of-the-way spot without too many distractions. I also remind them to bring their conference questions with them (the same questions I presented earlier in the chapter). The children are used to these particular questions, and the more they write and conference, the more they tune in to these specific areas and details.

I try to stress active listening skills during conferencing. When a child is ready to begin the conference, he or she reads the piece out loud to the listener. The listener can interrupt at any time when something isn't clear. In this way, the author receives immediate feedback about the writing which stresses that he or she has to be accountable for everything he or she writes. After the author has read the story completely, I let the partners talk with each other and react to it. Some examples of conversations might be: "You wrote a really great story," or "I enjoyed one part of your story a lot, but you need to explain in more detail about your adventure at the beach. You lost me at that part." After they've had a few minutes to talk, the listener begins to ask the author questions from the conference sheet. At this time, I insist that the listener record all suggestions for revising or editing. The sheet is then kept in the author's folder so the child can refer to it for the second draft.

At this point in using the process approach, I found that I was easily frustrated and many times wanted to give up on the idea of revising and conferencing. I think my frustration stemmed from trying not to tell the child how it should be written. My children frequently finished their conferences in less than ten minutes time and really had nothing to show for it. I would often hear the words, "Mrs. Miller, we've had our conference and nothing is wrong and nothing needs to be changed with Josh's story. He likes it just the way it is." I usually responded by saying, "Nothing *has* to be *wrong*, but could there be parts of the story which could be more exciting or more detailed?" At these points I realized, very quickly, that if I were to stick with the process, I would have to prepare myself for a long haul.

When I began using this approach with my class, I had preached to them about the author owning his or her story, that the author has the choice of changing or not changing anything in the story. But I found my own words coming back to haunt me whenever I, or another student, would try to influence a child to change what he or she has written. I was soon hearing, "But Mrs. Miller, you said we owned our stories and we didn't have to change anything if we didn't want to." These situations occurred much more often in the beginning of the year than they do now, since I have discovered the reason for this problem and a way of dealing with it. Many of the children's frustrations stemmed from the fact that they did not know how to make the recommended changes. Now, I have the author and the listening partner sit down with me and begin their conference again. At this time, I try to pinpoint any unclear parts and suggest ways the author can improve the story. Before too long, the author finds that he or she now has some strategies for revising without losing the feeling of ownership.

Just as I use myself as a third helper in conferences, I also use the children in my class as third helpers. If I find that one child is especially good at tuning into an author's story and making suggestions, I occasionally ask that child to help other writers. It's a good idea to pair children together who will profit most from each other. Although I often let the children pair up with a person of their own choice, I sometimes ask someone to conference with a specific writer because I know it will be to the author's advantage.

While the children are conferencing with each other, I am also a partner with a child. If I see that a few children aren't taking enough time to be helpful to an author, I will call some of them over to observe the conference I am having so they can see how we are going about it. This is a reminder to me that returning occasionally to a group conference can be helpful. Bringing the group together reinforces the ideas about conferencing that I've been trying to promote.

I also try to bring the class together two or three times a week after writing or conference sessions to vent our frustrations and to express and share their opinions. I had a child this year who told the class that she felt she was terrible in a conference because she found she was not really listening to the story. She felt much better when two other children admitted the same thing. We then began to think of some ways to make listening to someone's story a little easier. One child suggested that discussion should take place after the author had read a few pages. Another child suggested that the *listener*, not the *author*, read the story out loud. In this way, the listener couldn't get overly distracted if he or she was doing the reading. This idea seemed to work well for many of the children and I gave the class the option of doing it.

After a child has had a first draft conference, and I have checked the suggestion sheet to see whether suggestions to the author have been written down, I allow the writer to begin to make the changes he or she wants to make. I don't ask the children to copy over everything they've already written in doing their revisions. Instead, they work from their original copy, adding or deleting the details that they discussed in their conferences. We devised a few ways of revising which the children found especially enjoyable. One is by cutting and taping. Once the authors have decided which sections need to be expanded, they rewrite those parts and tape them onto the page. If a part needs to be eliminated, the child just cuts it out of the story and retapes the page like this:

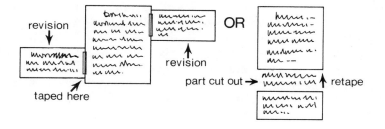

I find that the children like to take the time to cut and tape, and it relieves them from the sometimes tedious job of recopying. Sometimes the children choose another way, which I call pasting over. The author decides what needs to be revised and after making the revision, pastes it over the original.

The revisions that the authors make are what I call their *second drafts*. No copying over of the same piece has occurred, but much *rethinking* and *revising* has gone on in order to produce a more complete and enjoyable story. The rethinking that occurs at this time is one of the most valuable steps in the process approach. It proves to the author that writing and rewriting can be an ongoing process that improves a story.

Sometimes I have felt that second drafts didn't meet my expectations when I didn't see a lot of improvements on revised work. I have had to ask myself what I was most concerned with—the *end*, or the process toward that end. I have always chosen the latter. Many times I could have sat down with an author and told him or her exactly which revision to make, and how to word it so it would be acceptable to me, but would that have been fair to the child? The children, as writers, needed to feel a sense of responsibility for their stories, and to have the decision-making power regarding any changes. Decision-making is a valuable tool which I can stress in my class through this approach to writing.

When a child makes even the smallest revision, it can be a real breakthrough and provide a deep sense of accomplishment. An example that comes to mind is a story that Nathan wrote early in the year about his cat. The cat was missing. He started his story by saying, "I ran to my Mom to tell her I *knew* my cat Pete was missing." He went on with his story until the end but never told his readers *how he knew*. So I asked Nathan this question and he began to explain that his cat was kept in the playroom, where there was a screen door that had a big hole in it which led outside. He also told me that whenever he went down to see Pete, he would call him and Pete would meow and cuddle up next to his leg. I suggested that Nathan add these details to his story and he agreed that they would help to explain the unclear parts. This was the only revision Nathan made in his second draft, and even though I thought more could have been revised, he felt satisfied about adding what he did. This example confirms my conclusion that if the children can feel this sense of pride and *control* over their stories, they will continually want to keep revising and rethinking. After a writer has gone through the second draft revision, he or she reconferences with the same partner from the first conference, who is already familiar with the writer's story.

After an author has gone through two conferences, he or she comes to me for a proofreading session. This is usually the first time that I see the completed story unless, of course, I have previously had a conference with that child. I now check for several things—grammar, mechanics, usage, and the child's achievements of writing goals.

Writing goals are individualized for each child. Each month when I hand back each child's accumulated papers, I identify three or four specific problems such as forgetting capitals at beginnings of sentences or indenting when starting paragraphs, etc. The goals could also be more general, for example: trying to describe your characters in more detail, or describe your settings more vividly so your readers can see the places you are writing about. I write the goals down on a separate sheet which the children keep in their writing folders so that they are easily accessible. Each child is responsible during that month for checking for these goals in his/her writing. This system handles the frustrations of dealing with language skills and yet doesn't dampen a writer's desire to write freely.

When I sit down to go over the author's story to check language skills, I try to ask the author to point out the mistakes and tell *me* what needs to be changed. I'll ask the author what his or her goals are and if he or she thinks they've been corrected in the story. I then know that the child recognizes the errors. I may end up saying, "Joshua, you really forgot your goal of remembering to use capitals and periods. You need to go over the story and put them in." After Josh has corrected his story, I look at it again.

Once I have discussed the mechanics of a story, and whether the writer has achieved his or her writing goals, the child can choose to *publish* the story and make it into a book for our classroom library. The children get extremely excited about actually making their stories into a bound, sewn, hardback or paperback books, and the procedure they follow is artistic, fun, and relaxing. I have a table in my classroom known as the "publishing table," and all the supplies that the authors need are available to them in this area. When the children decide to publish, they recopy their stories or have them typed. The children are so anxious to see their stories bound into a book with illustrations that they don't seem to mind recopying. They use unlined 8-½" × 11" paper, which they fold in half. They make lines with a ruler so that they have guide lines when writing. The children can draw page-length pictures or add small illustrations at the top or bottom of pages. Most children love the opportunity to draw their favorite parts of their written stories.

The children will often go to the library to see what a book might also have in it besides the printed text. For example, a page about the author, or a prologue, or a chapter page. The children enjoy adding these parts to their books. It makes them feel quite professional!

When the pages of the story have all been written and illustrated, the children add one sheet of construction paper to the book and then sew the pages down the middle using the basic "back stitch." This sheet acts as a cover slip to be pasted down on the cardboard cover later.

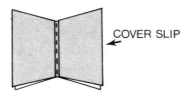

COVER SLIP

Sewn together here in middle of book.

Next, the children take two pieces of 9" × 12" cardboard and cover them with a sheet of wallpaper, or any available thin piece of material. I then take the two pieces of cardboard and put them side by side to tape them together with colored masking tape.

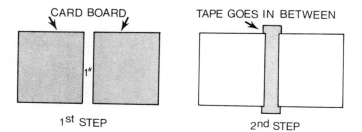

CARD BOARD

TAPE GOES IN BETWEEN

1"

1st STEP

2nd STEP

I am careful to leave at least an inch of space between the two pieces of cardboard as I place the tape to attach them. The final step is to put the sewn book into the cardboard covers. I do this by gluing the cover slip onto the cardboard while placing the middle of the sewn book on the masking tape which was put on earlier. This procedure may seem involved, but when done enough times in front of a small group of children, it seems easy—they catch on quickly and are soon helping each other "publish." If supplies are scarce and hard to find, I ask the parents for any they can contribute—scraps of material, needles, thread, cardboard—their response is good and they are glad to oblige.

The young authors are very proud of their published books. After decorating the covers, putting a copyright date on the inside, and identifying their book with a nonfiction tag and a number (for card cataloging purposes), they attach a sign-out card that they have made in the back pocket so that the children in the class can take the book out and enjoy it. The children love to see their peers signing out their books. It is a moment of glory for each of them.

Because the children love to share their completed publishing, I hold a special event at the end of the year. We organize a "Meet the Authors" party. At that time, parents, teachers, other school children, and our principal are invited into our room to meet and talk with the authors and to read their books. I arrange the classroom desks in a semicircle, and the authors sit behind their desks with their books in front of them. Many of them give "autographs" to anyone who asks. The children feel very special during this party, and many of them suggest we have more than one "Meet the Authors" party.

When an author publishes a new book, we add it to our own classroom library—these books are separate from our other paperback or hardcover books. The children often sit with each other during free time or reading time and enjoy each others' stories. The children also share their books with children from different grade levels in our school. Throughout the writing year, the authors in my class visit other classes to read their books. They really love this time and the feedback I get from the other teachers is very positive.

The children's growing excitement about writing, coupled with positive feedback from parents and other teachers, showed me that the process approach to writing was worth all the hard work and the frustrating days. It was always very helpful and very comforting to me to discuss this writing program with my colleagues, who were attempting, as I was, to make it "work." We often had grade level meetings or small group conversations so that we could better understand the many different facets of the process. It was a relief to know that other teachers were sometimes satisfied with the results they were getting from their writers and at other times totally distraught. It was during these times that I realized why the children in my class loved their sharing time during writing!

The longer I use the process approach to writing, the more I realize that children need to have an opportunity to become more independent in their thinking and acting. This writing program is one way of giving them the chance to begin to rely more strongly on their own decisions and judgments and to take pride in their own accomplishments.

4. Developing Independence: Sixth Grade

Cynthia Bencal

Getting Ready

I begin the writing process in my classroom early in the year in a simple and direct way. I tell my students that they will be doing a good deal of writing, and that through this, they will learn how to write better.

The process approach is not easy to describe to them, so I let the characteristics of this approach—the goals, methods, and the system we will use—unfold in formal and informal discussions over the first few weeks. We discuss the different types and purposes of writing, and the students offer ideas about why writing is important to them now and will be in the future. The students see their older brothers and sisters writing for college courses, and they accept the fact that they too are learning to write better by writing more. Together, we show that many of the jobs students would like to do require some kind of writing, and whether it is forms, reports, or memos, part of doing these jobs will mean being able to write clearly and specifically. They begin to see what happens if a reader does not understand their written ideas, for as readers themselves, they know that if a piece of writing is boring or unclear, they just don't read it. If they do not write clearly and well, either no one will read their writing, or those who do read it won't understand it correctly.

In class, students look at books of fiction to find writing that they like, and they discuss why it appeals to them as readers. We look for the techniques the authors use to produce good writing. In a good "word picture" students can find specific verbs and adjectives. In a catchy lead sentence or paragraph, they find either suspense, tantalizing information or inviting dialogue. They like crisp, lively detail and dislike wordiness. They like real characters; they see that these authors create characters who speak, act, and react honestly. From such discussions we begin to formulate general definitions of strong writing and weak writing. The students begin to use the words "clear," "focused," "descriptive," "detailed," or "specific" to describe good writing, and the words "unclear," "confusing," "general," "vague," or "wordy" to describe weak writing. I can then begin using these words and ideas as I discuss their own writing with them.

Then we discuss how writers improve their work and become more skilled at their craft. The one ever-present factor is the writers' willingness to revise and redraft their work. I use copies of various drafts of a famous writer's work so the students can see the "mess"—the work involved as the writer crosses out, adds, and rearranges ideas, and sometimes even scraps whole paragraphs.

Sixth graders are impressed with quotations from famous adult writers about the struggles of writing, so I give them a few: Ernest Hemmingway said that he rewrote the ending to *A Farewell to Arms* over sixty times before he was satisfied. Roald Dahl said, "By the time I am nearing the end of a story, the first part will have been reread and altered and corrected at least one hundred and fifty times. . . . I am suspicious of both facility and speed. Good writing is essentially rewriting. I am positive of this."

I tell my students repeatedly that part of writing better is learning how to help *themselves* to write better, that as their teacher, I could tell them what they should add to and cut from a piece, but that then it would no longer be their own writing. The first step in helping themselves write better is having material to work with: enough material to let them make choices about which pieces they will revise and redraft extensively and which pieces they will abandon; material they "care" enough about so they want to make it better, clearer, more exciting.

I emphasize the process over the product. This is a year for them to learn more about their writing, not to aim to create perfect final pieces from each idea. I say that there will be many times in the future when they and other people will only be interested in the final product of their writing, so for now they can be concerned with discovering the best ways for them to get to that final product.

Getting Started

Students can learn to write best by working with types of writing and subjects that are easy for them and natural to them. Journal entries and personal narratives describe them and their world, and this is what they know the best. At the start of the year, I ask students to keep a journal, and I give them a set time—ten or fifteen minutes, two or three times a week—to write entries. I supply them with a bluebook-sized notebook.

Journal entries are observations and reflections. Their purpose is to help the writer in some way—to remember an experience, to understand a person or situation, or to lead to ideas for more formal writing. I emphasize that the journals are for them, but that sometimes I will collect them. If they do not want me to read certain parts, or if they want me to respond, they can note it. There are no specific requirements for keeping their journals, although I encourage some to write more or to experiment with different ideas. Once in a while I will announce that if students have been using the journal only to record observations, they might also try to include their reactions to or feelings about an event.

Keeping a journal gets students writing often, if only for a short period. Letting them write about their lives and giving them school time to do it gives students the message that writing about their world is valid. It's important that students are able to write freely; since I feel comfortable not judging or correcting journal writing, or even not reading it, I can pass on that freedom to the writers.

Journal entries often give the students starting points for a personal narrative piece or later, for a fiction piece. Students may expand a journal entry about an event into a longer piece, or associate a phrase they have written in an entry with a person or time and begin a new piece on a related topic.

A personal narrative is different from a journal entry in that it stands alone as a piece that is planned and directed, although loosely directed at first. The piece is often shared with student listeners, student readers or the teacher, for their interest and their comments. This sharing can lead to a discussion that often leads to the writer's deciding to revise the piece. Working with personal writing has inherent advantages. If students write about what they know and care about, they will probably care about the writing too. If students write about their own experience, they will both remember the event and be able to write it in sequence. They can be helped to remember more details as interested listeners ask them questions such as, "So what did you do then?"

Fiction writing is natural to students too because it asks for stories. Some students have stories running in their heads ready to be told. Their reading is story reading too: most of my students choose to read fiction books in the popular genres. Given a choice, many sixth graders will choose to write fiction. They say, "Fiction is easier than personal writing. You can write anything you want. Your characters and plot can do anything. You can use your imagination: you don't have to rely on remembering true facts. Creating stories is fun."

They are right in some ways. At first glance, fiction writing is freer in offering unlimited choices for characters, plot, and setting. But because of these choices, it is writing that is much harder for students to control and improve, and thus feel satisfied with.

A piece of personal writing on the other hand has fewer elements for student writers to deal with than other types of writing. Facts, sequence, plot and characterization already exist, and so do not have to be researched, "thought up," or "made believable." If students are to try fiction or report writing in the future, it is better that they first practice some of the thinking and writing techniques they will need by doing a kind of writing that makes fewer demands. Therefore, I encourage my students to work with personal writing for two to three months before they begin fiction writing.

Prewriting

The assignment I give for personal writing is always, "Write about an experience you have had, or write about something or someone you know about and care about."

Prewriting for an assignment can start well ahead of the

writing. I tell the students about the piece the day before I assign it to them, so they can be thinking about it. On the following day, I may have them explain how they got their ideas. Prewriting thinking and prewriting activities can take place with the whole class, in small groups, between partners, or individually.

To help find topics, the whole class often brainstorms categories of experience, coming up with ideas such as, "an embarrassing time," or "a time I was scared," or partners can interview each other to help focus on a topic. If a writer has some general ideas, the interviewer can ask specific questions about the writer's particular interest, or about the experience itself. For example, if a writer has "dogs" for an idea, an interviewer may say, "Do you have a dog? What kind? Does it do tricks? Does it ever get into trouble? Oh yeah? Well, what did it do?"

In small groups, each writer can try out an idea, and members of the group can tell the writer what specifics they, as readers, would like to know about the idea. For example, if a writer wants to write about "camping in Yellowstone National Park," members of the group may say, "I'd like to read about Old Faithful. . . . I'd like to read about the bear or moose you saw. . . . Did you get scared at all? I'd like to read about that."

Many of my students perform prewriting activities individually. They reread their journal entries for personal narrative ideas or list things about which they might write. They sketch pictures to recreate a scene in an event they experienced. When students have decided on a specific topic, they can begin to find words and phrases to describe it. A technique my students have found helpful is to list the names of the five senses and under each any related specifics they can remember. If, for example, a writer's topic was "the time I learned to swim," he or she might list these specifics: *SIGHT*: black water, choppy waves, rocky bottom; *SOUND*: motor boat's hum, kids yelling from the raft, my own teeth chattering.

Partner and small groups activities are difficult to monitor in progress. They require discussion and therefore can be noisy. For good management of group work, I try to make sure the goal of the activity is clear to each group, to emphasize that the students are being asked to help each other, and to set a reasonable time limit.

Writing

Because the writing or composing process is really made up of many steps—thinking, prewriting, writing, sharing, revising, and rewriting—*writing* as one step in the process is difficult to separate out from the others. Writing is a personal activity, and within a few days each student is working at his or her own individual stage in the process. One student may have written three first drafts of three different pieces, have had conferences on some or all of them, and have decided to abandon them all and start draft one of piece number four. At the same time, another student may be working on the third draft of his first piece, having been helped by student and teacher conferences. It is exhilarating when a class of sixth-grade students works as writers and readers/listeners in this highly individualized way, but it can also be overwhelming to try to monitor. I will discuss such management issues later.

When my students write drafts, they use lined yellow paper and write in pencil for easy erasure. They skip every other line to give them space to add or rework. Because they may want a reader to read a draft, or because they may want to come back to a draft later, I encourage students to write legibly, and with as much correct spelling and punctuation as they can manage for draft work. Students must label each piece with the date, a title (or number) and a draft number, for example: Nov.1, Piece #3, draft #2. This way all their work-in-progress is together but can be easily rearranged or removed. When they finish a piece, they give me the final copy with all of the drafts. I keep this completed work filed in an individual folder for each student.

Writing Conferences

In my class, students share their writing with a variety of audiences—a student or the teacher, a small group, or the whole class—and at different stages in the process. Sharing prewriting ideas, sharing confusions, triumphs, and failures while writing, sharing various drafts, or sharing final drafts all fill specific needs of a writer-in-process. The students gain from experiencing as many combinations of these as they can because such interaction helps to create a supportive atmosphere for their writing.

One necessary part of sharing writing is having one-to-one conferences. The more conferences a writer can have with different people, the better. Each person is a different audience and will ask the writer different questions. The writer may begin to find his or her focus during one conference and be helped to remember details during another. As a teacher, I have skills that student conference partners may not have, but am I the only intended audience? My students need both teacher and peer conferences.

The wonderful thing about conferences is that they almost always succeed in some way. Most students do not need much to get them writing again if they are stuck, or to get them thinking an idea through if they are given another's perspective. A writer can do a lot with response like "That part is confusing," or "I like this paragraph the best." I find that student writers ask readers to do what they do well and like to do—respond naturally and honestly. And their responses help the writer.

Most students quickly learn to hold conferences with each other just as I hold conferences with them, so I try to set up the atmosphere and outline strategies for useful peer conferences right from the start. I teach the whole class how to have conferences by demonstrating the technique with one volunteer student. I sit beside the student writer and begin to read his or her piece aloud while the whole class listens. I stop when I have a real question about the content, either because something is unclear or because I would like to know more. I take about five minutes to complete a conference.

Sample Dialogue: T = teacher   S = student

T: (Reading student's piece.) "One day I thought I would really show my brother once and for all who was the most clever, but it all got switched." What do you mean "it all got switched"?
S: Well, my plan got turned around and it worked against me.
T: Oh, I see, it backfired.
S: Yes.
T: (Continuing to read.) "I made this scary mask out of papier

mâché and found some old material to make a costume to
scare him." What did the mask look like? Why was it scary?

S: Well, I molded these heavy eyebrows . . . then I made the
nostrils flare out. I painted on some bloody scars . . .

At the end of the conference I ask the writer, "are there
ideas you would add if you were to rewrite this piece? What
would you add or cut out?" These questions help the student
to remember what was said during the conference and to define
the next step by choosing from among many ideas.

I have at least three open conferences using the above model
during those first few days when I introduce the idea; then I
either have a conference with each remaining student in the
class, or I ask students to try peer conferences modeled on
mine. After everyone has had a conference, students revise—
and more importantly, they often choose to revise—their work
by writing another draft.

If a student chooses *not* to revise a piece, I usually honor
that decision. However, if I think a piece has a lot of potential,
I may coax a writer into spending time on some revisions by
reminding him or her of good ideas raised in the conference.
Those who don't revise a piece either begin a new piece or go
back and work on an earlier one.

Because student readers often ask the writers specific questions about content, I try to ask questions that draw out the
writers' ideas. I try to listen and react to what the writers say:

Tell me about this piece.
What part do you like the best? Why?
What part do you think needs work or discussion? Why?
What is the most important thing you are trying to say?
Did you give enough information about that idea?

I use my understanding of their style to share my observations with them. I may identify a technique or element, or
comment on what they did in a piece. For example: "Did you
notice that in this piece you chose to describe the building of
the campfire in detail? You chose to skip over the part about
falling out of the canoe." This type of comment may be enough
to help the writers clarify just what they *have* written and what
they *want* to write. From there, they can keep the original
focus or shift it.

If they do something well, I tell them what they have done and why it worked. This often leads them to look for other places in the piece where they could do the same thing. I try to react honestly. If I do not understand something, I tell them.

I use my judgment about how much direction to give to each individual student. Some students react best to the question, "Where are there places you could show us something, not just tell about it?" Other students need a more directed approach: "How can you show us how big the campfire was?"

As soon as student writers begin sharing their work, they risk losing possession of it. The student readers and I may have "lots of great ideas" for making a story better, but this changes the writer's role from writer—that is, one who owns his own work—to one who only carries out other people's ideas. This aspect of the writing process—the writer's possession of his work—is difficult to sustain, especially if a writer *wants* a reader to tell him what to do. It is most important at the beginning of the year to remind student readers to *ask questions about the content* of a writer's work rather than letting them *make statements about its quality* or *suggestions for its improvement.* To make sure I, as the teacher, don't take possession of a student's story, I try to keep in front of me the list of questions that draw out the writer's ideas first. To help writers take responsibility for thinking about their own writing instead of leaving it to a reader, I often ask them to reflect on their piece before they share it in order to translate one of their writing goals into a question for a reader. For example: *Goal*–"I want to give a good picture of how I fell into the water." *Question to the reader*–"Does this piece help you picture how I fell into the water?"

Before they share it with a reader, my students often try to write the answers to questions about their own writing, such as, "What is the most important thing I am trying to say? . . . What is the strongest part and what is the weakest part of this draft?" This way they come to a writing conference with some specific thoughts and opinions about their work, which can give the conference more direction and can give them a better chance of remaining in control of their own writing.

Problems and Frustrations—Classroom Management

The frustrations I feel with the process approach to writing stem from my own difficulty in giving up control in two different ways—as classroom manager and as editor. It is hard for me to accept that I cannot and should not read all that each student writes, and that I cannot always know who is at what stage in what piece. It is hard for me not to give direct suggestions and advice to a writer and not to feel that I should always be *teaching* "good writing" to the class. I have to work at controlling my tendency to want to edit and tell students what to write. Instead, I try to let the students share with each other, and make their own decisions.

To ease my frustrations as a classroom manager, I try to set up a writing environment that is serious and work-oriented as well as relaxed and respectful of the writers as individuals. Writing time means that students are thinking, conferencing, writing, reading for ideas or style, and making small or large decisions, and that they are doing this with concentration, effort, and productivity. They have the freedom to work on whatever specific step they are on, but they must be working on their writing, and they know they are held accountable. Sometimes I ask students to keep a log of their writing plans and accomplishments so that they and I can follow their process and progress. A log entry looks like this:

```
Day I _____(date)_____

My plan _____

What I accomplished _____

Plan for homework/tomorrow _____
```

If student-student conferences begin to be too long and I suspect, not too productive, I may ask students to record information about their conferences on one of several conference log sheets that are scattered around the room. These log sheets have the following information:

```
Writer _____Reader _____

Time of Conference:  From _____to_____

Decision(s) made: _____
```

These log sheets help the students focus their discussion and remind them that they are accountable for their time. At the same time, they provide me with information about students' writing and they help me regain a sense of general control over the work that is going on.

I take time to teach my students to use writing, editing and conferencing techniques in separate workshop sessions because I value the students' own ability to improve the quality of their writing as they experience writing as a process. By allowing students to help themselves and to help each other, I can ease my frustration at not being able to play the role of the "all-knowing" teacher/writer/editor. We also spend time examining fiction writing in books—looking at lead sentences, details, choices of adjectives and verbs—and in this way, students acquire a vocabulaty with which they can discuss their own and other students' writing. In workshops I may hold open conferences as conference training sessions, or I may give practice exercises that ask students to expand a paragraph by adding effective detail, or to rework a paragraph so it is more specific and concise. Practicing this way helps many students develop skills they can use in their writing. It gives them more ability to see where a sentence needs to be expanded, for example, and some background in *how* to do it.

Providing students with practice in writing techniques helps me to deal with my worry about taking possession of their work and to accomplish my goal of encouraging them to improve their writing through drafts. I am teaching them skills that are valuable and transferable outside of writing, and they are assuming the responsibility for applying these skills to their own writing. In doing so, they are learning to make careful decisions as they write, and I am learning to respect their ownership needs.

Another problem I have faced is in managing *my* time as a teacher during the writing sessions. I *like* to talk to students about what they are writing and thinking, and I often make conferences too long. To balance that tendency, I try to talk more with students while they are writing and not always to wait until they have finished a whole draft of a piece. I also try to walk around the room rather than sitting in one place and having students coming to me; having to stand while I talk shortens my conversations. And I ask students to come to their conferences prepared with questions or with their own opinions about their work. This helps us all to focus and shorten our conferences.

Drafting and Revising

Revising is the hardest and yet the most worthwhile step for writers. Writers make important decisions at this step as they synthesize their own opinions and ideas, their readers' comments and questions, and the techniques they have learned for improving writing. Revising can be rewriting a whole piece. It can be reworking the whole or redefining the focus of a draft. Revising can also be reworking parts of the piece, even just a few words or phrases. I try to let my students choose which of their pieces they want to revise, and often in making that choice, they are also deciding *how* they want to revise.

If I am having a conference with a writer, I try to gear my questions to where the writer is in the process. After draft one, a writer needs to decide if the piece has the focus, or emphasis, he wants. Does he want to continue to write about the whole three-day camping trip, or just about capsizing in the canoe on the first day? Does she want the piece to start at the point at which she cut her knee or does she want to back up and include details about the events and her thoughts as she rode the skateboard down the long, steep hill?

If a writer chooses to stay with one piece and carry it through successive drafts, my questions, the writer's plans, and the revisions will then most likely shift to concentrate on achieving a set of goals, such as "showing" not "telling" key parts, or including new action details in one part, or cutting some conversation, or tightening some description—in other words, the finer points.

I ask writers to have at least one conference with a friend, or with me after they finish a draft. Oftentimes that will spur them to revise, either because the conference showed them they should improve it, or the discussion of the piece rekindled their interest and reminded them of more details they wanted to include. Conferences help students see just how much perspective they have on their own work: to identify the strongest and weakest parts of a piece and explain why they think the way they do, to identify the main point or idea, the key sentence or paragraph, to evaluate the lead sentence, to see what parts of a piece they need to share with an audience to gain perspective.

Some students do better with written comments than with conferences. I often ask my students to write three or more questions that they would like a reader to answer about their piece. The reader then reads the piece and answers the questions in writing. The reader and the writer may or may not discuss the piece afterwards. Or, sometimes I will assign specific questions to the students who are acting as readers. I revise these questions each year. My goal is to develop questions that are helpful and supportive to a writer without taking away control over the writing. Questions I may ask a reader to answer are as follows:

> What do you think the writer is trying to say in this piece? (What is his or her reason for writing it?)
> What did you like best about this? (This can be an idea, sentence, description, phrase, word.) Explain why you liked it.
> Was anything unclear or hard to follow? What?
> Write down a phrase or sentence from the piece that gave you a good word picture.

I will sometimes ask students to go to their folders and choose one piece to revise or redraft. If I am teaching a specific technique, I may ask students to revise the piece using that technique—for example, to choose words and phrases that help set a mood, or to create word pictures so a reader can "see" the setting. At these times I will give specific assignments or exercises. If students are working on setting, I may group together students who have chosen similar places to write about. They brainstorm specifics to share based on sense perceptions. Each member contributes orally. If, three students are writing about a place near the water for instance, they would share SOUND specifics. 1) *Plink-plunk* of someone walking into water; 2) *Whoosh* of someone running into water; 3)the *slap* of drops of water thrown up, hitting the water again. The students keep a record of the specifics that could help them in another draft.

Mechanics, Grammar, and Spelling

I deal with mechanics and grammar during individual conferences in a very systematic way. At the beginning of the year, I tell the students that I will be looking at certain pieces of their writing (I tell them which pieces) to assess their strengths and weaknesses in mechanics and grammar. I do this using "Brookline's Composition Objectives for Grade 6," which I have included at the end of this chapter. I assess three pieces per student, and I write notes to them and to myself. I then give each student a list of these Composition Objectives in chart form, and the three papers I have assessed. We go over the rules for conventions, and then each student rates himself on his ability or strength in each skill.

I hold individual conferences with each student to determine which skills do not need work, and for which the student will be responsible; we then determine the skills on which the student does need to work by looking at the papers together and reviewing which rules a student has not followed or has forgotten. Together we determine one, two, or three competencies that the student will be assigned to work on. (The number assigned varies according to the newness and difficulty of the competencies for each student.) After this conference, when the students are writing final drafts, they concentrate specifically on their assigned competencies. Even then they can still ask for a quick review of a rule, or have me check a passage for correct use of those skills, or go over a practice sheet.

When the student has mastered these competencies by focusing on them in one or more pieces, he and I will determine the next set of competencies he will work on. I explain this procedure to the parents and keep them informed about which skill(s) their child is working on at any one point. This procedure for identifying competency problems takes a good deal of time, but it is worth it. Students do not become overwhelmed with mechanics and grammar in their writing, and their skills do get better.

I also teach short specific mechanics or grammar units to the whole class or to a small group. Over the years I have discovered that most of my students need review and practice in certain areas—using quotation marks, using commas, using

In the Middle : New Understandings About
Writing, and Learning
Nancie Atwell — (Eagle conon)

Coming to Know : Writing to Learn in the
Intermediate Grades
Nancie Atwell (Editor) Paperbook 1990
$27.00 — Bot ordered   LB 1576 .C578
Heinemann   1/11/90   Eyers   1990
IBSN 043508500X   Stel. 3
                                    Main deck

Side by Side   Paper   Syme to do Th M

0435-08586-7

apostrophes to show possession, beginning new paragraphs—so I will concentrate on these in mini-units separate from the writing time. As we go over these skills, the students try to use them correctly in their writing.

I always encourage students to try to use correct spelling in all of their drafts, because poor spelling often slows down or frustrates their readers. I let the students ask each other about spelling, or I will often spell out words for students. In each draft before a student's final draft, spelling errors are noted, either by me, a parent, or another student. The writer then has the responsibility to correct as many errors as he can for the final draft. The writer records any errors that remain in his final draft on his personal spelling chart, which he can draw from later for individual spelling study and work.

Publishing

I have not emphasized publishing as a special formal step in my class, although I plan to do that in the future. Until now, publishing in my classroom has meant that students choose a piece and take it to its final form. A published piece is written in cursive, in pen, and on white paper. The writer tries to make it as error-free as possible, with special attention to his own problem areas.

A parent or I myself often see the last draft before the finished piece, and we point out errors the writer has made relating to assigned skills. For example, if a writer is working on eliminating run-on sentences, I will often go through a last draft and write "RS" in the margin of the lines that contain this error. The student then is still doing the correcting, but has some help in where to look for problems.

For a published piece, I ask students to proofread two or three times and to read their work out loud to themselves. They proofread once for content, once to find and correct specific skill errors, and once to find general punctuation and spelling errors.

Evaluating

In Brookline, students receive grades for the first time in grade 6, so I am responsible for grading as well as making a general evaluation of the student's writing. The criteria I use vary somewhat according to the time of year and type of writing, but there are some general categories which I always use in my evaluation. I share these criteria with students, and in fact, they often evaluate their own work according to these criteria. I usually ask the students to choose the work they want to submit for a grade. The work needs to be something that they have published. They submit all drafts in order and any notes, reader's sheets, and self-evaluation sheets that they used in the development of that piece. I then follow the process they have gone through, read the drafts and notes in order, and assign them four grades: on the final piece, the process, how well they performed in their assigned skill areas and on their general skills and spelling.

I grade the final piece according to standards of good writing, looking for those elements that the class has worked on together. If we have talked about good leads and specific detail, for example, I will give a higher grade to writing that has included these elements. In this way, as the year goes on, and we discuss and practice more writing techniques, the criteria for a higher grade become more demanding and writing improves.

The process a student goes through is difficult to grade. I look for the student's effort and true involvement in a piece. Has the writer used the time well? How willing has the writer been to take an honest look at his work, to revise, to experiment, to seek conferences and to use the information from them? Do the drafts show work and growth? There is no easy formula for evaluation in these areas. Sometimes draft 2 is worse than draft 1, but draft 2 shows the writer experimenting. Can the writer then use these experiments to go on and better develop his ideas? Evaluating revisions is hard too. Some writers need to do a major revision on some pieces; others need to do a good deal of fine tuning, so the basis for evaluation is the quality, rather than the amount, of revising that is done. The evaluation of the process is a process in itself, which takes practice. Walking through the drafts of a piece with each individual student, and having him explain his thoughts, decisions, and goals along the way might be the best way to understand, and thus evaluate, a writer's process in his writing.

Using a process approach to writing at the sixth-grade level is never easy. The teacher must maintain a classroom atmosphere that is at once supportive of self-direction and experimentation, and also accepting of time restrictions, grades, and specific goals. What the students have to say, and their styles of working, writing, and sharing are the things that shape the writing class. It is hard for a teacher to know just where individual students and the class as a whole will go. Like anything with a life of its own the process approach is different every day: some days are terrific, others are horrible. Some students seem to progress as writers, others to regress. Sometimes the writing is great; sometimes it is poor. In the same way, my style of teaching writing is changing and evolving. I am getting better; I know I have a way to go. But I don't mind being at this stage; it is easier to relax in my own learning process when I know that my students are "in process" as well.

The process approach is not the easiest way to teach writing, but to me it seems the best way. I used to keep much more control over my students' writing and revising when they wrote stories for me. I would guess that over four years' time, I owned about 800 stories, from which I leased parts to my 200 students. *Some* students learned to write better. A *few* learned to write well. *Too* few experienced writing as a process for themselves. It is different now. My students own their own stories. They like to write. They are writers now and best of all they want to continue to be writers when they grow up.

Composition: Skill II
Composition Objectives: Grade 6
The student's written composition will demonstrate the following:

> **Basic Competencies:***
> G/U 1. Capital letter at beginning of sentence.
> G/U 2. Capital letter at beginning of proper name (including days of week, months of year, place names.)
> G/U 3. Capitalization of titles.
> G/U 4. Period at end of declarative sentence.
> G/U 5. Question mark at end of interrogative sentence.
> G/U 6. Comma in dates and place names.
> G/U 7. Comma between elements in a series.

G/U   8. Use of quotation marks and commas when reporting direct speech.
G/U   9. Apostrophe in contracted words.
G/U 10. Indentation of first word in paragraph.
G/U 11. Elimination of run-ons.
G/U 12. Elimination of fragments.

Additional Competencies:*
G/U   1. Apostrophe to show possession.
G/U   2. Verb tense consistency.
S   3. Consistency of speaker's voice.
G/U   4. Agreement of subject and verb.
G/U   5. Comma after introductory phrase or clause.
S   6. Elimination of repetitive connectors, e.g., "and" and "then."
S   7. Use of appropriate transitional words and phrases, e.g., "however" and "after."
S   8. Appropriate use of a variety of sentence patterns.
S   9. Sentences placed in natural and logical sequence within a paragraph.
S   10. Use of examples, evidence, or details to support generalizations.

*Competencies are coded G/U for grammar and usage skills, or S for stylistic skills.

5. Creating An Atmosphere Of Trust: Grades Seven And Eight

Evelyn Lerman

The method a teacher uses to implement a process approach to writing with junior high school students depends largely on the experience the students have had in the lower grades. If they have been exposed to the process for a number of years, as described in previous chapters, they slide quite easily into it. If, on the other hand, they are used to the "student writes, teacher corrects, student copies over" model, they may feel threatened by this method. Being "right" matters a lot to this age group for grades are an important part of their school experience. Time is important as well, because they may have as many as six or seven subject teachers, each of whom requires papers, projects, and other homework. Since this approach calls for a relaxed attitude about both grades and time, this could become a source of conflict between teacher and students.

The first step, therefore, in introducing this method to students who are new to it, as well as to students who have used it in the lower grades, is to establish an atmosphere of trust. Student must believe that though grades will be given, they will not be given after each draft. Teachers must believe that what students have to "say" in their writing matters more than the ultimate grade. Patience must follow closely behind trust. Being "right" may be a long way off in the first draft, since the emphasis in early drafts is on clarity and focus, with succeeding drafts dedicated to sequence, specificity, and finally to polished syntax and clean mechanics. Everyone must be prepared for hard work and deferred gratification.

Once it has been established that the process approach will require trust and patience, the teacher can begin to introduce the rationale for using it. A method that has worked well for me with students as young as ten and as old as thirteen has been to start by asking, "When you have something important on your mind, something you know a lot about and care a lot about, and you want someone to know about it, would you rather write about it or tell it?" This begins an interesting discussion about the benefits of writing, the benefits or talking, and the disadvantages of each. Some observations students have made may be of interest:

"Talking is easier. You never run out of tongue."

"Writing is safer. You can throw it away without anyone ever having heard it."

"Spelling and handwriting slow me down. My mind rushes faster than my pen. In talking I don't have that problem."

"When I write, I can't tell how my reader feels about what I am saying. When I talk, all I have to do is look at the person. I can tell if I'm telling it right."

"In writing I have only words, sentences, punctuation, underlines, and possibly italics to help me get the feeling across. In talking, I have all of the words and sentences AND I can shout, stamp, bang on the table, whisper, grunt, and use my whole body to make my point."

"When I hear myself talk, I know what I said."

"It's hard to think when I'm writing because the act of writing gets in my way."

"You might want to change what you said on the paper and it might be too late. There are no 'ers, ums, I means' to help you when you write."

"I'd rather write. I can reflect, change my mind; I can hold my hand back, but my tongue runs away with my mind."

Each time I have had this discussion with a class, a few students have said that they prefer to write, but the overwhelming majority that they prefer to talk. Writing is seen as inhibiting, slow, and, for some, even painful. After a class has had a thorough discussion of these ideas, and students have heard from each other, it's a good time for the teacher to explain how the process approach recognizes these problems and offers writers a chance to use the benefits of writing and talking, while eliminating some of the disadvantages.

Good writing often has some passion to it. The first assignment I give the students, therefore, is to write on a topic they know and feel strongly about. A class period can be successfully spent brainstorming ideas. Since strong feelings can be positive or negative, and for adolescents, negative feelings can be threatening, it is important for the teacher to be aware of and sensitive to problems students may be having in selecting topics.

Once topics are flowing and students have begun to record them on the front cover of their writing folders (a management system I will discuss later in this chapter), writing can begin. Students should be encouraged to write on one side of the paper only, thus allowing the opportunity for later cutting and pasting instead of rewriting. They should let the writing flow and not stop to look up words or ask about them. If a writer feels uncertain about meaning or spelling, suggest he circle the word for later discussion. Crossing out is encouraged; concern with punctuation can wait. Let the writing come, just as if the student were talking; even "ers" and "ums" are fine at this time. When the writing flow begins to slow down, and the writer feels the need for discussion, this is a good time to introduce the conference.

Conferencing Is The Most Difficult, Yet Most Valuable, Step

I have found conferencing to be the most difficult part of the process approach, though every teacher I know who has used this method of teaching writing agrees that it is the most valuable. Successful conferencing can result from any of the following: teacher/one student; teacher/small group of students; teacher/whole class; student/student; small group of students. One problem here is that of management, since writers must have relative quiet in which to work, and students who are conferencing must be able to talk with one another. The noise level must be a successful compromise, which is the hardest for students to achieve. The second management problem is the variety and availability of movement. A successful match of enough freedom and enough responsibility requires a high level of student/teacher cooperation and awareness. Though difficult, it is attainable, and from the perspective of the results, worthwhile.

An even more difficult problem for the teacher in conferencing is playing the role of listener and helping the writer focus and clarify. Even more removed from the experience of the traditional teacher of writing is the role of observer and "orchestra leader" when students conference with one another. Having to put my editing pen away, and learning to ask questions to help the students become their own editors were teaching styles so new to me that once I made the leap, I viewed myself as a "Born Again Teacher of Writing." I must confess that there are still times when I slip back into my old habits.

The new way of approaching a student's writing calls for no more "do this, do that, fix this, change that." The conference is the setting for asking questions that show interest in content and encouraging the writer to try for more successful communication. The attitude of the listener is accepting and interested. The difficulty here is obvious to teachers because, in addition to being accepting and caring, they must also strive for better student writing. Accepting everything as wonderful or brilliant and crying tears of happiness over a piece does the writer as much disservice as accepting nothing and bleeding red ink all over the paper. Both blur the writer's perception of himself as writer. The teacher's role is to be helpful by motivating the writer to achieve better focus, clarity, sequence, style, and mechanical integrity.

The advantage of the conferencing class is that, unlike the traditional class in which the student is expected to write "the" rough draft and "the" final draft, it establishes the attitude that all pieces of writing are drafts until the writer decides it is time to publish. Questions such as:

Which part did you like best?
Why did you run away at that particular moment?
How did you feel when the tent collapsed?
Where do you want to add more details?
Is there any part you want to take out?

sharpen the writer's sense of what he wants to communicate, and motivate him to redraft once more. He is not correcting errors; rather he is continually improving his writing. There may be as few as two or three drafts between conferences or as many as a dozen.

But the number of drafts is not the major difference; the attitude toward drafting is. The writer doesn't go from "all wrong" to "all right." He goes from initial attempts at focus and clarity to revision and further attempts. A conference might deal with a paragraph or the whole piece. The important aspect here, and the real point I want to make, is that the student has no sense of failure because he is reworking his paper. He is not doing something over; he is doing something differently. Revision is "looking again," and that's what the conference enables the writer to do. He looks again and hears again through the eyes and ears of his reader.

To make lighter work of the actual redrafting, and to use the writing period time to its best advantage, I suggest to students that they put their efforts into writing and conferencing, not into copying over. Given a shelf full of inexpensive lined, yellow paper or recycled white paper, scissors, pencils, and Scotch tape, students write on one side of the paper only. After a conference, the writers cut out lines they don't want, write new lines, rearrange the order, all with the cut and tape method that does away with rewriting anything that may become a permanent part of the piece.

You may notice that I use the word "piece" when referring to the writing. This is deliberate so that I will not use the word "story," as I have found that writers think "character, plot, and setting" when they hear the word "story," but are free to think about mood, description, moments, sensory perceptions when they hear the word "piece." Since we are looking for jewels of writing when we begin this process rather than strung-out necklaces, the "piece" allows more freedom. It also allows the writer to use the criteria, knowing and feeling strongly about, with more flexibility.

Words which the student has circled in early drafts are addressed during the conference if they come up during the question and answer discussions. Writers are helped to choose words which are more specific, more dynamic, clearer or more effective. If the words have been circled for spelling help, they will be corrected if meaning is affected. "Were coming" does not mean the same things as "we're coming," but "jepardize" does not affect the reader's understanding, though it may affect his sensibility if he is an English teacher. In final conferences, however, all remaining spelling errors will be considered inappropriate, and will be corrected by the writer.

The student needs a place to keep his ideas for writing, his materials, his work in process, the work he decides to stop working in, and the work he decides to publish. In the past I have thought about this as a folder, flat and filed. As I continue to work with students on the writing process, I begin to see this "place" as a portable writing desk. Perhaps it should be a large box in which the writer can store all the material he needs to work with, as well as a place in which he can keep the folders. In addition, he could use it to write on, choosing the place to work, either in the room or outside when weather permits. Keeping two folders for each student seems to work best in my class. One is labeled "In Process," the other "Finished." The "In Process" folder holds all the work on which the student is working. This seems clear to them from the beginning. The "Finished" folder takes a little more explanation. This is for work about which the student no longer cares. He has worked it over, but he has not worked it out. But, since he may want to revisit it at some future time, he keeps it in this folder. "Finished" means that the paper is not, but the writer is, at least for now. When the writer decides to publish, he takes his work out of "In Process" has a polishing conference, and follows it by making a final, public copy.

Explaining this folder system often brings me to the model of the Process, which I share with students and will share with you. If it looks suspiciously like a flow chart from a computer class, that's because I was taking such a class at the same time I was teaching the Process to both teachers and students. It looks like this:

Model of Writing Process

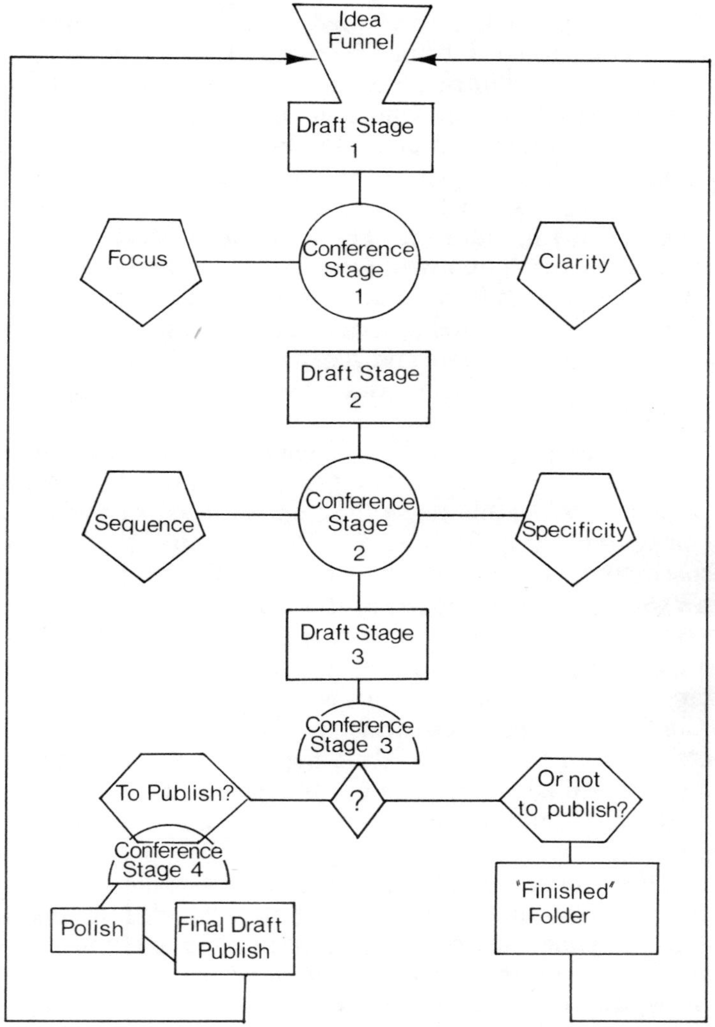

Each writer's Idea Funnel, which comes from class brainstorming and individual or group thinking, musing, observing, and dreaming, needs to be stored somewhere. A convenient place in a classroom is the inside cover of the In Process folder. Our students were intrigued by a famous author of children's books, Robert Cormier, who told them that he had an idea bank in the bottom drawer in his desk. When he needed an idea he went there to pull out old menus, matchbook covers, used envelopes, and whatever other scraps of paper he had used to record his idea on. There he had words, phrases, a character's name, a quote—anything that he liked and thought worth saying. This is the purpose of the inside cover of the folder; here is the writer's bottom drawer. The place doesn't matter as long as it is safe and accessible. As the model shows, this is the place the writer comes back to when he has either "finished" a piece, or published a piece.

The drafting blocks and conferencing circles on the model are labeled "stages" to indicate that the number of drafts and conferences is flexible depending on the need of the writer. Some writers jump Stage 1 because their first pieces are so focused, they are so sure of their topic, that they can spend time with the reader ordering thoughts and becoming more precise in their selection of words, phrases, or syntax. Other writers may follow these stages exactly, while still others may jump back and forth between them.

Conference Stage 3, the decison block, is a moment of truth. Now the writer must decide whether to go public and invest himself in a final copy, or to put the writing aside and start a new piece. Should he decide to publish, and this can be anything from submitting it to the school paper to putting it on the bulletin board, from turning it in for a grade to taking it home to his parents, he must now polish his writing to a fine sheen. I explain the need for this extra effort by pointing out that it is the courteous thing to do in order to free the reader to enjoy the meaning. Poor handwriting, incorrect spelling, faulty mechanics, and crumpled paper detract from the content. The analogy which younger students enjoy is that of eating in the kitchen with the family compared with dining at the Ritz. If you go public you have to scrub your hands harder, comb you hair, change your clothes, sit up straight, and keep your elbows off the table. This makes you appropriate for a public place. So it is with a published piece. Its appearance on the bulletin board, between the pages of a homemade book, in the local or school newspaper, or at home for parents makes it open to public view. It has to be clean, neat, and technically correct. This means white paper, ink, margins, legibility, and of course all mechanical aspects correct.

But there is more than courtesy involved here. It is also an act of closure for the writer. He has completed a piece with pride and is ready to start the process again. There is also closure here for the teacher, who will revel in a beautifully completed piece of work. And the parents, seeing the results of much effort, will add their commendation for both writer and teacher.

The experienced teacher of writing, and indeed the experienced teacher of any discipline will immediately ask, "What about the student who never selects publication?" The teacher knows whereof he speaks. Falling through the cracks is a skill which otherwise inconsistent students have mastered with great consistency. The teacher must set limits for these students. These could be a number of published papers due within a given period of time or one paper due after a few are written; the teacher, knowing the student, will devise a system to overcome the avoidance behavior. Actually, it is not always possible to overcome it, though sometimes a teacher can circumvent it. The best motivation is to find out what genuinely interests the student, and direct the writing toward that. A teacher-friend of mine, who was a "pro" at twenty-five when I was a novice at forty, once said to me, "When in doubt, ask the kids." If it seems a hard decision to make in your classroom, ask the writers to suggest limits they think would work for them while not inhibiting the process.

Grading, mentioned briefly at the beginning of this chapter, is an important, and very difficult issue at this level. Seventh- and eighth-grade students are ambivalent about grades. They want them, seeing them as proof of their abilities and efforts; yet they feel constrained by them when trying to work out problem situations such as a process approach to writing. Grades are seen as prizes for the competitors. Winners get A's and losers get E's. In a situation in which the teacher expects the usual bell curve, the students are aware of this and expect the usual rules to apply. But this approach does not lend itself easily to such grading for many reasons. There are a number of questions to be asked. The first of these is *what* to grade? Should students select their own piece for grading? Should they turn in a package which contains all the drafts together with the final draft? Should drafts be graded along the way or should grades be saved for published work only?

The next question is *how* to grade? Should the teacher use the bell curve, comparing one student's work with another's? Though this problem is no different than that facing the teacher of writing in the traditional setting, somehow it seems different. Perhaps it has to do with the student's view of ownership of the piece. It has been established from the beginning that the piece belongs to the writer, with the reader, including the teacher, acting as interested observer. If the teacher now says "A," the student reads, "I knew I was doing good work all along," but if the teacher now says "C" or lower, the writer reads, "This paper is awful and all the work I did on it was a lie. If it was good enough to redraft all along, why is it now so bad?" One obvious resolution to this dilemma is not to grade, but if grading is the expectation, the teacher does have to devise a workable system. One solution for my class was to devise an evaluation form together, students and teacher, establishing criteria for grading. A point system completed the form. It looks like this:

WRITING PROCESS EVALUATION

CONTENT	POSSIBLE POINTS		POINTS RECEIVED
CLARITY	14		_____
FOCUS	14		_____
SEQUENCE	14		_____
SPECIFICS	14		_____
COHERENCE	14		_____
MOOD	14		_____
Possible Total	84	Your Total	_____

MECHANICS			
SPELLING	4		_____
PUNCTUATION	3		_____
VERB TENSE AGREEMENT	3		_____
PARAGRAPHING	3		_____
TRANSITIONS	3		_____
Possible Total	16	Your Total	_____
		Your Grade	_____

Evaluator(s) _____   Writer _____
_____   Date _____

This evaluation system lends itself to a view of grading which is different from the traditional view, for the teacher and student are really working on each writer's work as a separate entity. There is no room here for comparison; each writer is being evaluated according to his own production, which fits in well with Benjamin Bloom's theory of mastery learning. In his latest book, *Human Characteristics and School Learning*, Bloom says that sensitive systematic instruction, combined with enough time and assistance as well as clear criteria of what constitutes mastery, will make it possible for about 80% of all students to achieve the level of achievement ordinarily graded A, a level usually reached by only 20% of the students. This insight helped me a great deal when I realized that I was giving so many A's and B's in this process, compared with other units of study in which the bell curve nearly always came true.

Who grades? Each class can make its own agreement on this. Some possibilities are: the teacher grades alone, the teacher and the writer grade, a group of peer editors grade, each working independently, and averaging the grades when finished, or any combination of the above.

Why grade? If the teacher buys the notion that grading is valuable, some reasons to back up this position are:

1. Students need a formal evaluation to validate their efforts.
2. Teachers need grades because the system requires them.
3. Teachers need grades to validate their efforts.
4. Parents need grades to feel they know what their children are accomplishing in school.
5. Grades are motivators of hard work, both on the part of the student and the teacher.
6. Grades create the image of hard work; lack of grades create the feeling of play.

The Process Approach Is Worth The Effort And Frustration

The reader of this chapter has by now grasped my point of view. I like the process approach. I believe in it. I see the results. I also see problems and I surely have experienced frustration. If you plan to try it, you will probably appreciate some of the problems you may be facing. Time is the first concern in trying to work through this curriculum. In a typical

Junior High School English class the teacher is expected to devote time to reading, literature, speaking, listening, study skills, research skills, and writing. Fifty minutes a day is little enough time to devote to all aspects of the Language Arts, but when the teacher makes a commitment to the Writing Process, time becomes the biggest obstacle. Ideally, students should write every day, preferably at the same time of day. The teacher, if free to write along with them, adds a rich dimension. This makes it infeasible to have conferences about anything but the writing, and the time becomes a total commitment. Some classes give a specific period of time to the process at the beginning of the year—four to six weeks—and then use it throughout the year as needed. Others work with it for two weeks, leave it to work on other curriculum, and then return to the process throughout the year. The interesting result is that as students become proficient at being their own editors, their skills transfer to other areas such as report-writing, speech-writing, debating, fiction-writing, science work, social studies, and so on. The teacher, worried about the excessive time being spent, now has justification as transfer takes place. I am even beginning to believe that the writer who has internalized the process becomes a better reader because he begins to think like the writer. His skills in literary analysis and comprehension grow as his skills in expression improve.

A second source of possible frustration is attitudinal. Students, accustomed to being given assignments which they write, turn in, and receive back with a grade and comments, may have a hard time believing a process approach is real work, and hard work at that. They may also have difficulty sustaining interest if grades are their only motivation. Although we would like to believe that learning is its own reward, many students and their parents do not accept that as enough. Motivation may suffer, causing the teacher to have to work very hard to set a mood in the classroom in which genuine effort is expended, and the rewards are writing improvement, interaction, and results. Frequent conferencing, either with the teacher or with peers, oral sharing of student writing, and lessons with the class or smaller groups on specifics of writing help to keep motivation high. Successful publishing is the best motivator, with creative types of publication serving as a showcase for completed work.

Students' egos, fairly fragile at this age in all cases, may suffer during conferencing or during topic selection time. If a student feels free enough to choose a topic about which he really cares, and is then "put-down" in any way about it, he may withhold this type of sharing from then on. The sensitive teacher will establish an atmosphere in which ideas and effort are valued and privacy is respected. Questioning must be the result of interest and involvement rather than implied criticism. Redrafting must be the norm rather than the exception. The most effective device I have found is for the teacher to use his writing for public conferencing and subsequent redrafting. No amount of suggestion to students or discussion about the process works better than the open conference on a teacher's draft in which the whole class participates. The teacher's attitude about students questions establishes the tone.

Parent understanding and support are vital, and not always forthcoming unless the teacher makes a genuine effort to keep parents informed. Because the process produces fewer than usual papers, because the number of grades may be sparse, and because papers may go home with few markings on them, appearing uncorrected by traditional standards, parents may begin to worry about the writing curriculum. This is an area of such importance that another chapter in this book is devoted to it.

Are the mechanics considered of so little importance that they come last and are forgotten? This prospect can be frustrating to teachers, to parents, and frequently to students. The philosophy which guides the correcting of and attention to mechanics is the same as it has always been for teachers of writing. I believe that a painter cannot paint without an understanding of his tools. Neither can a writer write without understanding grammar, usage, punctuation, spelling. These are tools of his trade, but only some of them. The ability to focus on a topic, to clarify the topic, to write a piece that has good sequence, to produce writing that is specific enough, yet general enough, these are the essence of the canvas. The ability to put the ideas together masterfully, to create sentences that are varied and polished, to punctuate and spell correctly, these are the techniques of brush stroking, highlighting, matting and framing. The finished piece of writing and the finished painting both reflect all of the skills. The difference here between the traditional mode and a process approach is the timing of the emphasis on mechanics. Lessons are taught throughout as needed to explain the fine points of grammar, syntax, punctuation and spelling, while the conferencing in Stages 1, 2, and 3 centers on the heart of the piece. By the time the writer has reached the point of publication, most of the syntactic and grammatical problems have been solved through the clarification of meaning. The remaining spelling and minor punctuation problems are corrected in the polishing conference, and now the teacher is merciless. The published piece must be letter perfect. The message to the writer in this process is that meaning, style and, mechanics follow each other in sequence. Mechanics, rather than being devalued, are elevated to a status of great importance. Publication is not possible unless the student makes every effort at perfect proofreading. In our classroom we staple a "Basic Competencies Writers' Proofreading Sheet" to the back page of the In Process folder. The writer and reader use this to help them spot and fix all mechanical errors. Spelling dictionaries are also available for spelling errors. If the teacher continues to sense anxiety on the part of any of the participants, including himself, he can do an analytic evaluation of a draft for each student about once a month, using the proofreading symbols the class has agreed upon. He returns this to the student, who then records the results in his Writer's Competencies Record, which shows his progess throughout the year.

I conclude this chapter with the student comment I included earlier, which said, "When I hear myself talk, I know what I said." What I would say is, "When I see what I wrote, I know what I think." Writing this chapter has cleared up a number of problems for me, by affirming my belief in the process approach, reaffirming my observation that the work is demanding, and convincing me that this method works.

WRITER'S COMPETENCIES RECORD

THE SENTENCE	MINIMUM COMPETENCIES						
C	Capital letter at beginning						
P	Period at end of declarative sentence						
P	Question mark at end of interrogative						
RO	Elimination of runon sentences						
FR	Elimination of fragments						
MECHANICS							
C	Capital letter at beginning of proper name						
C	Capitalization of titles						
C	Quotation marks for direct speech						
P	Comma between elements in series						
P	Apostrophe for contractions						
P	Indentation of first word in paragraph						
STYLE							
S/V	Agreement of subject and verb						
	ENRICHMENT						
THE SENTENCE							
SP	Appropriate use of sentence patterns						
RP	Elimination of repetitive connectors						
TR	Appropriate transitional words						
MECHANICS							
P	Apostrophe for possession						
P	Comma after introductory clause, phrase						
STYLE							
VT	Verb tense consistency						
VE	Voice consistency						
GEN	Reduction in generic words, i.e., "said"						
SEQ	Sentences in logical sequence						
SUP	Examples, evidence to support generalizations						
	PROCESS APPROACH SKILLS						
	Focus						
	Clarity						
	Sequence						
	Specificity						
STUDENT CODE:							
1.	I do this well and consistently.						
2.	I do this sometimes.						
3.	I do not do this.						
4.	I don't know what this means.						

6. Explaining The Writing Process Approach To Parents

Evelyn Lerman

Once a teacher of writing becomes committed to the process approach to writing, it would seem that he should be ready to pursue this rigorous curriculum. He has examined his own philosophy of education, he has reached out to his students, he has adapted his methodology. Surely he has done enough. But, there is yet another job to be done. He must inform and educate the parents, so that they, too, become his partners and support the new curriculum.

The basic difference between the process approach and that of the traditional writing curriculum is so significant that the task of informing the parents of this enormous change warrants its own chapter. The reader who is a teacher will immediately recognize this necessity, for parent support has always been an important part of the successfully run classroom.

If we look at this approach first from the parents' point of view, we will see that their children are bringing home fewer papers, while those papers which they are bringing home may be "in process." To the uninformed eye, they will appear uncorrected, messy, neglected by the teacher. The parent will rightfully begin to worry about a writing class in which the teacher and students appear to be doing so little work. If we look next from the student's perspective, we see that the teacher is telling him that, when revising, it is acceptable, he is even encouraged, to cross out, circle, cut, paste, add, and subtract, while his parents may be telling him that such work is careless and not acceptable. The teacher sees himself as an educator who is attempting to instill writing habits and attitudes in which he believes while finding his credibility questioned or even attacked outside of the classroom. It is, therefore, to the benefit of all participants that the rules of the game be made clear. Parents give their support once they are made aware of teacher goals; students give theirs when they are not getting mixed signals from school and home.

The following outline of the information parents need is brief, since the content of the process approach has already been explained at length in the various chapters:

1. The process approach derives from educational research and the observations of writers.
2. The class is process-oriented rather than product-oriented. Therefore, finished work will not be as frequent as parents may expect.
3. The work of the curriculum is in focusing, writing, editing, clarifying and revising, followed by final polishing which centers on spelling and punctuation.
4. During the writing, the student has conferences with the teacher or with other students. He then revises his piece, using their suggestions and questions to guide his changes.
5. Papers which appear to be "uncorrected" are "in process." The writer is working on a revision of this draft, based on a conference he may have just had.
6. Letter grades, when applicable, will be given for some papers and for the course, but not all papers will be graded.
7. Parents can help support this approach by talking with their children about their ideas, encouraging them as writers, and being patient while waiting for finished products.

The teacher can communicate this information to the parents by letter, (samples of which follow this chapter), during parent-teacher conferences, at an Open House during which student work-in-process is exhibited, at a demonstration class in which students are working, or through the school newsletter. The method does not appear to matter as long as the message is clear. Parents are needed; their support is valued by the teacher and the students. If the teacher is fortunate enough to have parents who are themselves writers, he will find that they are often pleased to come to class to talk with students about their own work, their trials, their successes, and the process of writing in general.

Two sample letters are reproduced overleaf. The letter on page 98 is recommended for upper grades (6, 7 and 8) and the one on page 99 is recommended for primary grades, especially kindergarten and grade 1.

Dear Parents:

We have just begun to use a process approach to writing in our language arts class. This approach is based on research conducted at the University of New Hampshire by Dr. Donald Graves. The Language Arts Department in our school system has suggested this methodology to teachers because the research shows that student writing improves as students use this method. In addition, we have found that students' attitudes toward writing improve consistently and that they become more positive about writing. I am sending you this letter so that you will understand the process approach and support your child through the difficulties as well as rejoice with him or her over successes.

The essence of this approach is that students "own" their writing. They are responsible for drafting and redrafting their work until they complete a piece which is focused, clear, sequential, and specific. It must, at the end, be neat, clearly written, correctly spelled, and perfectly punctuated. The writing is initially based on material the students know a lot about and care a lot about. Once students learn the process approach they are able to transfer it to other genres, with excellent results.

The heart of the process approach is the conference, during which students and teachers read, reread, discuss, question, clarify, and edit. The student/writer (and often the teacher/writer) take the draft back to the desk and revise according to the understandings reached during the conference. During the revision process, writing is scratched out, cut up, pasted together, rearranged, and so on. Copying over or writing over is discouraged; genuine revising of material is encouraged.

Letter grades will be given for the course and for some papers, but not all papers will be graded. It is hoped that the interest the student has in completing excellent pieces of writing will be motivation enough.

I will appreciate your bearing with us during this work, as you will be seeing fewer papers than you may be used to, and those papers you do see may appear to be uncorrected. This is because students will be working on "in process" papers revising their work as a result of a conference they have had on it.

The intial thrust is on selection of topic, focusing, clarifying, then sequencing and specifying. Once the student has accomplished these, he may then decide to "publish" his piece. Publication can take the form of being put up on the bulletin board, being taken home, becoming part of the school paper, being sent to the local newspaper, being turned into a book, or any other creative idea a student may have. In this case, he does a finished product which is edited and proofread until it is letter perfect. Should he decide not to publish, he goes on to choose another topic and begins the process over again. I will, of course, watch carefully to see that no student consistently begins over without having some closure on finished work.

Your support is essential to the peace of mind of the program, to both your child and to me, for one of the key ingredients of this process is that we all feel relaxed while writing; your support will help us to do a good job.

If you would like more information, kindly send me a note, call the school, or drop in to visit. I welcome your interest.

Kindest personal regards,

Dear Parents,

The book your child is bringing home today represents a process of beginning writing, now in use in the Brookline Public Schools Language Arts curriculum, called "invented spelling." There are several stages in this process, which starts with the representation of a word with a single letter. It gradually progresses to the inclusion of several letters per word, eventually adding vowels and all the correct conventions of spelling and grammar. Within a group of young children all stages are represented. The aim of the process approach to writing is to allow children the freedom and confidence to express themselves without being concerned about how readers will view their finished work. As the children add to their knowledge of spelling and grammar usage through the Language Arts program, their "invented spelling" will accommodate this increased information.

Later in the spring, the children will continue using this approach. In addition, several of their best writing pieces will end up as "published" selections which will contain correct spelling and conventions.

If you have any questions about this process, please feel free to contact me and I will be glad to elaborate on the procedure.

Yours sincerely,

7. Supporting Change: Staff Development

Naomi M. Gordon

Staff development has been an essential part of teachers' understanding and use of the process approach to writing. Through staff development work, curriculum administrators in the language arts department and teachers have worked together to improve established and effective practices. Although each school system has its own requirements, constraints, and procedures that need to be honored, a review of our thinking, planning, and implementation may give other teachers and administrators ideas that will help advance their own staff development work.

This chapter describes what we did from two perspectives. The first, "Dynamics of the Staff Development Process," explains the general approaches and values that shaped our meetings and their content. The second, "Specific Components of Staff Development," describes what went on in the actual training sessions. A look at our staff development from both of these perspectives conveys the context of our work.

I. Dynamics of the Staff Development Process

A Long-term Commitment

I want to emphasize that *staff development for a process approach to writing is lengthy and time-consuming.* Implementing this approach demands a long-term commitment from both teachers and administrators. Research on effective educational change in general, and curriculum and staff development in particular, consistently tells us that the one-shot workshop makes very little difference in teacher behavior. What works best are repeated sessions with some kind of "coaching," which then lead to substantive change and growth in the instructional practices of teachers.

The amount of staff development time needed for the change

to a process approach to writing is even greater than the amount needed for many other curriculum changes. Usually a curriculum change is supported by texts, kits, A–V materials, or other purchasable, external, tangible resources. The process approach as described by the teachers in these chapters, however, relies on *people* resources, specifically, teachers' increased understanding of writing as a process. It relies on their ability to ask questions, to pace their comments, to think fast, to relate with ease and conviction to parents, to individualize instruction, to take risks and learn from mistakes, in short, to depend mainly on themselves. Even for the strongest teachers, this kind of teaching requires support, or coaching, both from administrators who can tolerate problems, false starts, and weak moments, and from other teachers who are encountering similar dilemmas. This understanding and skill can only develop from *repeated* interaction with other professionals.

Our task was not to develop an approach to the teaching of writing: the process approach to writing was, in fact, a curriculum that had already been developed. Our major task was to *asssist teachers in developing their ability to implement this writing curriculum.*

Strong Administrative Support

Closely allied to a long-term commitment to the program is the quality of administrative support. In Brookline, the administrative staff of the language arts department was responsible for the direction of the writing program. We believed in the process approach to writing, said so clearly and often, and said so to a variety of audiences. We spent substantial amounts of time planning what to do, doing it, and following up on what we did.

The process approach was almost always on the agenda at our weekly administrative staff meetings. We shared our thinking on how to structure a meeting for teachers, on how to help a particular teacher who was getting discouraged, on how to communicate what was happening in a single grade level to the grades above and below. At first, we had relatively long discussions. However, as we built up a background of experience with these types of concerns, and with the teachers involved, we found that we could review an issue and make suggestions to each other in much less time.

There was some risk for us as administrators in devoting so much time and visible commitment to the process approach. In the beginning, we were not sure that the result would be an instructional improvement that would be evident to others. After all, we did not necessarily expect tangible results, such as higher test scores, but we did expect increased satisfaction with the teaching of writing for teachers and students. We thought that the process approach was a significant movement in language arts instruction, and as such, that it warranted our attention.

Administrators outside the language arts department were informed about our work on the writing process. The Assistant Superintendent for Curriculum and Instruction, Dr. Louise Thompson, supervised all curriculum areas. Dr. Thompson was interested from the outset and understood the value and importance of our work. She supported it by asking thought-provoking questions, making constructive comments, and by generally encouraging us. Fortunately, subsequent administrators, such as Superintendent Charles Slater and Assistant Superintendent for Curriculum Pat Ruane, have also been advocates of the process approach. Their prior knowledge and continuous support freed us from the necessity of reexplaining the process and convincing them of its value.

In our school system, curriculum department administrators have primary responsibility for curriculum development and for the staff development connected with it. Therefore, the principals were not the initiators of or primary leaders in our work, although they were, of course, informed about the process, invited to meetings, and could see the process in action as they visited the teachers in their classrooms. They also saw and approved the communications about the process approach from the teachers to the parents. Their responses ranged from neutral to positive. Recently, a prinicpal asked me if candidates for a job opening in the school had used the process approach in their former teaching positions. The principal's question indicated to me that he saw the process approach as an established part of the language arts program in the school. In school systems where principals do have a primary responsibility for curriculum development, their role would be analogous to that of our departmental staff; that is, principals would assume responsibilities such as planning and leading meetings, bringing consultants to the school, locating reading material, and supervising the curriculum implementation.

Collegial Relationships

One of the most striking aspects of our work with the process approach was the development of collegial relationships between teachers and administrators, relationships in which the participants were equal partners working together to solve problems of mutual concern and interest. In our case, the overall problem was how to put the process approach to writing into practice in a variety of classrooms. We had to search together, not for one way, but for many ways to interact with students and to plan instruction that would allow each teacher to put an individual stamp on the teaching of writing. These collegial relationships were perhaps a natural outgrowth of a situation in which all participants were learning together to understand and implement a new curriculum.

It took time for teachers to trust that this "new position" was not part of a plan, an instructional package, or a preconceived notion of what they should be doing. Indeed, we were not sure about the directions that the classroom program would take; teachers had to discover those for themselves.

Gradually, a sense of trust increased among us. As a curriculum administrator, I came to believe that teachers would not perceive my tentativeness and my failed hypotheses as weaknesses. Teachers came to believe that I would not perceive their uncertainties and their anxieties as weaknesses. We were able to share problems, to probe together to see what was going badly, and to plan some possible solutions. A teacher could say, for example, that she found it almost impossible to be as nondirective as the process approach seemed to require. We might then focus on possible strategies that would provide enough structure to make her comfortable. One suggestion might be to use a form for students to fill out during peer conferences. This would serve as a checkpoint, a way for the teacher to know what had occurred during conferences. Or perhaps I might have a demonstration conference with a student, and even if it went nowhere, I could feel it had been helpful for the teacher to observe; we could analyze the conference together to see where I had missed some opportunities, and to come up with some alternatives for next time. My early fear had been that if the curriculum administrators were not sure enough of our ground to have lots of firm answers, teachers would not stay with the process approach. This was not the case. Everyone's confidence and skill grew from the support we could give each other as colleagues.

There was another positive consequence of the collegial nature of our work. Just as we came to trust each other, we came to trust the students. We saw that the students did not give up when we did something "wrong." They kept trying to get something out of class periods and interactions that we perceived as weak and unproductive. They knew their teachers were struggling with something new, since their teachers often reminded them of that fact. Teachers frequently used class sessions to review aspects of the process. They shared their concern about students' difficulties in keeping work organized or having peer conferences. They shared their own difficulty in finding enough time for individual conferences or in getting first graders' books in published form. Students liked being part of a joint effort and having to rely on themselves as well as on their teachers. My conclusion is that the students began to relax in the same sense that we did, and this relaxed spirit strengthened and improved their ability to write.

An Optional Undertaking

The shift to a process approach was not mandated for teachers. Those of us who were on the language arts staff made it clear that we hoped teachers would try it, but we did not insist. Our writing program was not in trouble. There was no need to force teachers to change from their current effective instruction. We reasoned that teachers would be more willing to work as hard and as long as this change in writing instruction would require if they could choose to participate. We also thought that some teachers would find the process approach more congenial to their general teaching style than other teachers. Thus, a self-selected group would start the use of the process approach in our school system.

Our strategy was based on the hope that a relatively small

group of teachers would become involved and that their success, enthusiasm, and knowledge would spread to other teachers. Part of our role would then be to provide ways for our "experts" and subsequent beginners to get together and learn from each other.

Our strategy worked! The process approach continues to spread. Admittedly, we give it a large boost each year during orientation for the few teachers new to the system by describing the advantages and widespread use of the process approach. We also pick up on any show of a teacher's tentative interest in the approach and spend time with that teacher. But we don't force it.

After three years, it is possible to state that all our teachers have been influenced by the process approach to writing through some aspect of our staff development. But it is realistic to say that our staff development effort is not yet over. Teachers experienced in the approach continue to refine their work. We continue to look for new ways to help teachers get started and to assist others in making more use of the approach.

II. Specific Components of the Staff Development Process

Many considerations entered into the planning of specific staff development programs. First, there were the established methods for conducting staff and curriculum development in the system. Second, there was a need to be flexible and creative in focusing on the process approach. If we saw a problem, we looked for a way to solve it. Finally, we wanted to review and monitor the outcome of our sessions. We asked teachers to write evaluations of each meeting, and we took these documents seriously. This combination of following customary procedures, listening hard, and adding new procedures gave our staff development process balance and verve.

Meetings for Teachers

Our school system had an in-service plan for staff development in which curriculum departments held hour-long meetings for teachers after school—either grade-level meetings in each curriculum area, or optional special sessions offered at the discretion of the curriculum departments. We made consistent use of both types of meetings. During each of the past three years, the language arts department has organized approximately twenty in-service meetings dealing with the process approach to writing. Teachers would find half of these meetings pertinent for a particular grade level. My estimate is that teachers who implemented the process approach attended at least six sessions in their first year.

1. *Grade level, systemwide sessions.* The established structure was an advantage since teachers were accustomed to gathering in separate grade-level groups of about twenty people to hear and think about developments in each curriculum. Our introduction of the process approach was, therefore, not as special or as threatening as it might have appeared if a new format were used. It seems wise to follow a school system's regular format for bringing new curriculum development to the attention of teachers.

These meetings were planned carefully, and a variety of training techniques was used. Usually, we started by briefly explaining the process approach to writing in a general way and including a few theoretical references. Then we did a demonstration in which the group tried some part of the process. For example, at one meeting, we individually wrote a list of topics for a few minutes. At another meeting, each person listed and then narrowed a range of topics, and then wrote three possible leads for a piece on one of them. At still another meeting we brought samples of student work and held a model teacher-student conference. Pairs of teachers then conferenced with each other using student work as the material for their conferences.

At each grade level meeting, any role-playing replicated what could be done with students at that grade level. Teachers were asked to select topics that they knew about and cared about and to write as they would normally write. We did not attempt to role-play as our students, but to understand some of the issues facing them through our role-play at tasks they might do. Another summary of the process approach comprised the last part of these grade-level sessions. A general statement followed by a specific exercise and then by a second statement proved a workable plan.

The process approach is amorphous and complicated enough

to require that teachers experience it themselves before it becomes clear to them. The exercises served to increase the level of understanding so that the concluding review brought some closure. Questions and comments from teachers were encouraged during each part of these meetings. Our answers tended to be short and were sometimes deferred if the answer would be included in a later part of the presentation.

Frankly, we made some mistakes. We were so close to the topic that we went too fast. Although we may have been beginners in using the process approach in classrooms, by the time we held these meetings, we were not beginners in understanding what the approach was about. We had to keep reminding ourselves that nearly all the teachers were coming to this as something new and that they had not planned the meeting with us. In an hour's session, no matter how terrific an hour it was, we could not get across all the background information that we had gained in our many hours of thinking and planning. Gradually we slowed the pace, and questions from teachers were given lengthier and more immediate answers. We realized that later, second comments would work as reinforcers, and were not an unnecessary repetition. Teachers seemed to learn more and enjoy it more when we tried to cover less material at each meeting.

The results of these grade-level, first year meetings were uneven. At each of them, a few teachers became interested and excited enough about the process approach to want to try it. Most meetings left many teachers interested, but not quite ready to try to implement the approach. They seemed to have a positive, yet a wait-and-see attitude. A couple of the meetings left teachers wary, with a skeptical, if not a negative, "let's see what happens to those who try it before we do it" attitude. It was this last phenomenon that puzzled and troubled us. We tried to find plausible explanations. Although our meetings each had had a slightly different emphasis depending on the grade level, they had also, after all, been similar. Why such a varied reception to the ideas? After a great deal of appraisal and reappraisal, we decided that some of the differences came from something we could not control—the subtleties of group dynamics. Such factors as the initial spoken reactions of a teacher, teachers' other preoccupations at the time, and how the language arts staff was perceived in general may have contributed to the outcome of these meetings.

Teacher evaluations were valuable in our review of the meetings and as a basis for subsequent planning. When teachers said that this approach was what they already did, we knew that either we had not been clear, or that they had not been listening. In both cases, we had to try again. Teachers' comments on what had been helpful and what they needed to know more about suggested directions for later meetings and also for individual follow-up. An individual conference or a short meeting with two or three teachers during lunch break was often a good way for someone from the language arts department to address some of the issues that the teachers' evaluations raised.

We tried to learn from our mistakes and to remain positive instead of becoming unduly discouraged. This was not always easy at the time, since we were so eager and enthusiastic. We could understand caution; criticism was much harder.

The process approach to writing was the topic of the grade level language arts meetings for two years. By the second year, teachers had begun to use the process approach in their classrooms. Some of these teachers gave presentations at meetings: they described their writing programs and told how they had gone about incorporating the features of the process approach in their teaching of writing. These meetings were uniformly more successful and exciting than those in the first year. The audience now had more background. Teachers had seen and/ or informally heard from colleagues who were using the approach. Most teachers had attended the meetings in the first year and had read the articles that we had distributed. Some had even been to meetings at local universities or to professional conferences where they attended sessions on the process approach. Although some teachers were still skeptical, and others thought this approach was not for them, they all came to our next meetings wanting to hear more about an approach that was working in some of our classrooms and receiving attention at professional meetings and in professional journals.

If our audience knew more that second year, so did we. We on the language arts staff became more precise in our remarks. We could zero in on what was different in those classrooms that were using the process. We had specific local examples to share, which included examples of children's writing and of interactions with children during writing time in our classrooms. We no longer had to rely on experts from outside for validation.

I think that the teachers appreciated a second year on the same subject. In Brookline, administrators are prone to try to cover lots of ground and set lots of things in motion at once. At times, ideas and strategies may not get the extended attention needed to make them understandable and workable. Staying with the process approach as the major topic for our meetings for two years showed that the language arts department understood and respected the complexity of implementing this process. And we certainly needed this continued emphasis.

In the third year, the grade-level meetings continued to deal with the process approach, but in different ways. We focused on specialized aspects of the approach. Since teachers were already implementing the process approach or could learn about it at optional meetings and from colleagues, systemwide sessions on the approach in general became outdated.

With third and fourth grade teachers, we explored the relationship of drawing to writing. Jan Olson, an art teacher, had been working on visual narrative and its connection to writing. She described for us how drawing at many stages of the writing process can add depth, detail, clarity, and pleasure for students who are visual learners. Drawing had, of course, been used in connection with writing, but mainly in the prewriting stage for beginning writers. Now we explored a range of ways to use drawing as a "writing" exercise at different stages and with older students.

At other grade-level meetings, topics such as incorporating the process approach in writing research reports, genre units, fiction, and poetry were addressed. The writing connection remained, but the focus changed to meet the needs of our increasingly knowledgeable staff.

2. Multi-grade, optional meetings. Different types of meetings were held as optional sessions to follow up on the grade-level meetings. One format we used was to hold one or two sessions to focus on a particular problem for a particular group of about six or eight people who had expressed a shared concern. Although these sessions were open to all teachers, usually only the people who had raised the issue at a meeting or in the evaluation of a meeting attended. For example, teachers from contiguous grades met to brainstorm ideas for getting started with the process. Management issues and time allocations were topics of other informal problem-solving sessions. For the early grades, the rationale for invented spelling was an important topic, and teachers shared the ways they had discovered to use invented spelling as a basis for instruction and the letters they had written to parents to explain the process. The intention of these optional meetings was to provide small-group learning situations for teachers. They were short-term and each had a very specific focus.

The Support Group

Another format for optional, multi-grade meetings was the Writing Process Support Group. In years two and three, a group of about twenty teachers met regularly to discuss their progress with the process approach. While all teachers were initially asked to join, those most heavily invested in implementing the approach attended. Additional people were welcome at any time.

Exchanges such as the following occurred among the teachers at support group sessions:

"Some of the kids' writing is so bland, truly boring, and I don't know what to do about it."

"Right. I get some papers like that, too. They're logical, accurate, focused, technically fine, but dull, dull, dull! Yet, the kids are satisfied."

"OK. I know what your mean, too. But what can we do to help liven them up, get some details into them that will inform the reader, illuminate the ideas? As you say, they're so pleased with themselves, I don't want to appear overly critical and pushy. Especially when the pieces are theirs. We know all about ownership."

Gradually a notion crystallizes as alternatives are offered. We recognize a common problem and try some hypotheses. Perhaps these students tell uninteresting tales in general in their conversation as well as in their writing. Perhaps they are not thinking deeply, divergently, playfully. We push further.

We may need to focus more attention on colorful detail in whatever we are investigating, talking about, reading. We may need to develop more complicated, probing questions about events or people that are being described or read about. Perhaps the route to livelier writing for some students is not only in reviewing and reflecting on their writing. They may also need to be led to examine and reexamine their own ideas and feelings and to consider a variety of viewpoints and motives about all facets of their experience, both in and out of school. After all, good writers are persistent, keen observers.

This kind of conversation took place halfway through the second year of our support group. But it was not always like this. At the start we centered on survival skills—how to organize the folders, what to tell parents, and TIME. Time was a powerful obstacle: how to find enough of it to let the students explore the possibilities of topics, to write, to conference. Giving more time to writing meant having less time for something else. Even if the time formerly given to seperate lessons on skills and vocabulary development were added, the process approach demanded more time for writing than ever before. Teachers shared their guilt about shortcutting other subjects and slowly agreed that it would even out in the long run.

Another problem area in the beginning was what to do with all those pieces of paper. We showed each other folders for current work and folders for completed work or one folder with pockets for each. We decided that the main thing was to have a clear way to organize the papers and to make sure that every student knew and followed the system. We admitted that it was worth spending a chunk of precious class time on this seemingly peripheral task.

The question of the individual teacher's self-concept was another thread running through the early meetings. Almost every teacher was concerned that he or she might not be able to carry out this approach, that the quality of the students' writing would suffer. The approach seemed to require new and impressive skills. Whether stated directly or not, the presence of this self-doubt was clear. We openly acknowledged its inevitability; we offered reassurance to each other; we shared disappointments and failures. A helpful insight slowly emerged: the process approach for one teacher need not be a replica of the process approach for another. Indeed, it might not work if it were. The fact that the process approach began to work also helped teachers to overcome their self-doubt. Students did write at least as well as before, and some seemed to be writing more complex, intriguing pieces. A few weren't, but they hadn't been doing much writing before starting the process approach either. More students were able to experiment with language, to assume control of their writing. Some became remarkably sophisticated in their understanding of the process of writing and were willing to work very, very hard to meet their own new, higher standards.

Conferencing also emerged as a central topic. Scary at first, it became fun for us to try different groupings, to go back to a strategy that had failed a month ago to see if it would succeed now, to try someone else's technique for having the students develop questions or to include a checklist as part of conferences. We never outgrew our preoccupation with writing conferences. As the conferences improved, we thought about improving them still further. This is not surprising since the heart of a conference is thinking about how writing can be improved, a preoccupation which was always at the center of our work.

The logistics for the support group sessions were simple. We chose a day of the week and a time of the month for the meetings. I sent reminders. Mostly we met in our classrooms, but sometimes we met in our homes. Attendance was optional, but, as it turned out, regular. When people missed a meeting, they were usually filled in on the session by a friend and could easily contribute and learn more the next time they came. Occasionally there was a specific agenda or plan. For example, we might write and conference on our own work for a couple of sessions. Or we might limit the discussion to a single topic such as how to deal with the weakest writers or how to challenge the strongest. Mainly, we simply brought what was on our minds at the current stage of our involvement with the process. And something always was.

These comments give the flavor of our two-year-old support group and its concerns, a pivotal, and for us, a new component of staff development work. The other components that have already been described, or will be described later in this chapter, were important, instructive, and enjoyable. But we had learned from excellent consultants before. We had read instructive articles and heard presentations from language arts staff and other teachers at many in-servie meetings. The department staff visited classrooms often and interacted with students. What those occasions did not give us was the chance to get together repeatedly and informally and collegially to grapple with the same instructional issue—and the process approach to writing is an instructional issue that requires grappling with.

We did not expect that these meetings would continue for so long or be such a useful part of staff development. One explanation for their fruitful longevity is that the support group functioned as a study group. The members examined the writing behavior of the students, the intervention of the teacher, and its results. As we became seasoned in using the process approach, the sessions stayed lively and fresh because the quality of the writing and the tenor or the interactions of teachers and students advanced. We still learned from reflecting on the issues of the moment.

In addition, the support group combined the characteristics cited by research on staff development as key variables: The participants trusted each other. There were multiple sessions. The members chose to attend. There was time for reflection. And the members felt that their teaching practice was improving and that they were benefiting from the process of staff development. They were also enjoying it!

Classroom Visits and Demonstrations

Visiting classrooms and discussing instructional issues with teachers are routine events for administrators in our school system. Although less routine, demonstration lessons are also customary. Teachers and administrators often go over children's writing together, either to review progress and the possible reasons for it, or to deal with lack of progress and figure out possible ways to overcome the problems. These individual opportunities for staff development were frequent and valuable, especially while teachers were beginning to use the process approach.

Teachers might ask for an administrator visit to focus on students who had trouble gettng started during each writing time or to talk over ways to manage large group sharing of writing. A frequent request was consultation on the issue of conference strategies, including pacing teacher-student conferences and organizing peer conferences.

Teachers wanted to know the perceptions of another adult who understood the process approach. Often we simply confirmed or restated what the teacher had been thinking. This function of making explicit what teachers were doing strengthened their understanding and security and enabled them to continue more easily on their own. As helpful and frequent as these interactions were, they were minor in terms of the time the teachers spend alone with the students. Therefore, the cutting edge of whatever we did was whether it informed the teachers' independent instruction and contributed to their ability to analyze their own work. We also encouraged teachers to visit each other's classrooms whenever possible. The few teachers who made visits found them valuable.

Demonstration lessons took place at teachers' requests and at the request of the language arts staff, who wanted firsthand experience with the process approach. One model I used was that I would introduce the process approach in a classroom by teaching the opening lesson and then would return weekly for several weeks to coteach for a writing period. This gave the teacher assistance during the demanding first few weeks with the process approach, and it gave us both a common background of experience so that our subsequent consultations could be shorter and sometimes not include additional observation.

At times, demonstrations focused on a single one-time task. I might have a conference with a talented writer who thought his or her work was acceptable on the first draft and did not see any point in revising. Or I might role-play in a conference with a teacher to set the stage for peer conferences, or have a conversation with a student about why his or her work was going badly.

This sounds easy and natural as I write about it now. At first, however, it was hard for me to do these demonstrations. My investment was large. I wanted the teachers who had gotten this far to continue. I wanted the demonstration to be successful enough to insure that teachers and students were comfortable with the process approach. Mostly, although not always, this happened. What defused my anxiety was the realization that my demonstration was *not* the center of the process approach universe. Some demonstrations went well and the teacher still remained reluctant. Others went poorly—the students were restless; only a few wrote as well as they usually did—but the teacher forged ahead. I learned in a powerful way that my involvement was a part of a whole cluster of factors, some outside my immediate control, that would or would not make the process approach viable for a teacher.

Outside Contacts

Links with people outside the school system added strength and support to staff development. At first the language arts staff looked to these outside experts as key resources to explain and assist in implementing the process approach. As we progressed in our understanding and self-assurance, however, we relied more and more on ourselves. The outside researchers and authors remained important, but their roles shifted to that of colleagues and fellow explorers.

These contacts also supplied the evidence that the process approach was expanding elsewhere and becoming a mainstream method for writing instruction in elementary schools. It was a very satisfying experience to be among those involved with this approach in the early stages.

Consultants

Through a series of coincidences, members of the language arts department first heard of work on the process approach to writing in separate talks given by Dr. Donald Graves. We were then able to arrange a consultant session with him to make sure we understood the instructional implications of his research. The introduction to this volume reviews our rationale for instituting the process approach. In terms of staff development, the small group conference with Dr. Graves was itself a pivotal experience for the language arts staff. He answered many questions and confirmed our determination to bring the approach to the attention of all Brookline teachers.

Lucy Calkins, then working on a research project with Dr. Graves at the University of New Hampshire, led two sets of workshops for teachers, in grades three and four, and grades five and six. About a dozen teachers attended each set of three sessions that were held in the first year. These teachers were all making some adaptation in their approach to the teaching of writing. Ms. Calkin's workshops allowed them to ask questions of her and of each other as well.

In the second year, Sue Rotundi, another consultant, gave workshops for fifth and sixth grade teachers. Teachers in these grades had questioned taking the time to make a risky change when they already had a carefully wrought writing program and faced heavy demands in all curriculum areas. The classroom experiences at Atkinson Academy that Ms. Calkins had described occurred mainly in the lower grades and seemed more logical there. We therefore asked Ms. Rotundi, a former sixth grade teacher, to meet with us. She shared student work and showed us how the process approach could be used in many types of writing in these upper grades.

Recently, Brookline teachers and language arts department staff have been asked to give presentations and workshops on the process approach. These experiences are both an endpoint in our staff development and another beginning, because they stimulate us to refine our own procedures as a result.

Site Visits

The proximity to Brookline of the Graves and Calkins research site in Atkinson, New Hampshire was a bit of luck. Three of us on the language arts staff visited Atkinson Academy in October of the first year. The classroom observations we made through the arrangement of Jean Robbins, the principal, dramatically reinforced our belief that the essence of what was happening there could happen in our classrooms with noticeable results. Seeing real teachers with real students was a strong impetus. The visit inspired us to start and encouraged us to persevere through many bumpy moments.

We immediately arranged for Brookline teachers to visit Atkinson. The first available time was April! Although we had wanted an earlier visit, this timing turned out well. The twelve teachers who went had already started to use the process approach and had a background of personal experience for their visit. They were able to see some of their own strategies working in another place, get ideas for some alternatives, and confirm that some problems and issues persist even for those experienced with the process. They were also able to see that variations in how each teacher uses the process are inevitable and salutary.

Outside Reading

We distributed articles by the New Hampshire researchers on their work to Brookline teachers. These articles by Donald Graves, Lucy Calkins, and Susan Sowers, became our reference books. We read them before meetings, again before implementing the process approach, and again after doing so. Although the articles were short, somewhat anecdotal, and light in tone, their content was weighty. Rereading them at different stages in our own learning about the process approach let different parts of their message become clear at the right time. We continue to read and circulate journal articles on the process approach. The publications of the National Council of Teachers of English, the International Reading Association, and *Learning Magazine* are regular sources. From these we get more ideas and information and become more aware of the widespread endorsement of the process approach among language arts educators.

Naturally, as more work is published, reading and discussion will increase. Currently, our main reference books are Graves' book, *Writing: Teachers and Children at Work*, the Northeast Regional Exchange's book, *Understanding Writing*, and papers shared by Shelley Harwayne of the District 15 Writer's Workshop in Brooklyn, New York.

A Concluding Reflection

As our work on the process approach continued and we started to work on this book, we began to see striking parallels between our approach to staff development and the process approach to writing. For example, the teachers review and rethink what they are doing to teach writing. They consult and confer, they listen to others. But they decide what to change and how to change it. They control the "revision" of their teaching. Similarly, the students using a process approach to writing consult, confer, and listen to others as they review their work. But the students *themselves* also decide what to alter, what to leave alone. They are in control, they own their writing.

Once we started to think along these lines, the analogies came quickly. Neither writing nor staff development can be rushed; neither always goes well; neither gets stale if it is done well. There are always new issues, new problems to solve, new ideas to explore. Student writers and their teachers, as well as teachers and staff developers or curriculum administrators work best as colleagues who trust and respect each other, their knowledge of their craft, and their ability to make sensible decisions about how to improve their work. Both processes become more comfortable with time, although neither ever becomes simple. The list of similarities continues to grow as we continue to grow. Acknowledging them has added to our understanding of both the craft of writing and the craft of teaching.